The Gospel According to
Cannon & Ball

Also by Chris Gidney and available from the Canterbury Press

Dora Bryan's Tapestry Tales
Britain's best-loved comedy actress mixes personal reflections and favourite readings in this heart-warming and extremely entertaining memoir.
978-1-85311-621-6

Little by Little
Syd Little tells the inspirational story of his life on and off the stage.
978-1-85311-595-0

The Little Book of Heavenly Humour
A collection of all-time favourite religious jokes and cartoons by Syd Little and friends.
978-1-85311-543-1

Available from all good bookshops
or our website, www.canterburypress.co.uk

The Gospel According to Cannon & Ball

With Chris Gidney

Cartoons by John Byrne

CANTERBURY
PRESS
Norwich

© Chris Gidney 2007

First published in 2007 by the Canterbury Press Norwich
(a publishing imprint of Hymns Ancient & Modern Limited,
a registered charity)
13–17 Long Lane, London EC1A 9PN

www.scm-canterburypress.co.uk

British Library Cataloguing in Publication data

A catalogue record for this book is available
from the British Library

ISBN 978-1-85311-792-3

Typeset by Regent Typesetting, London
Printed in the UK by CPI Bookmarque, Croydon, CR0 4TD

This book is dedicated to all those who struggle with life and question their faith.
That's just about everyone then!

Introduction

Having known Bobby and Tommy for over 20 years, the one thing that has always struck me about each of them is their individuality and uniqueness. This distinctiveness is what has placed them above many other comedy entertainers and earned them the right to be hailed as Britain's kings of live comedy.

Anyone who has had the privilege of watching Cannon & Ball on stage will know how their own brand of humour reaches across the footlights and quickly gets the whole theatre rocking with laughter. When you get an opportunity to see the boys in a Gospel Show setting, however, it's fascinating to see how easily they manage to mix comedy with their Christian faith in a way that makes a belief in God both exciting and relevant for today.

This book is a wonderful example of how Bobby and Tommy see life and faith from a different perspective. These two hardened, northern welders were probably the last candidates on earth you'd expect to embrace the Christian faith, but included here is the story of how two fervent spiritual cynics eventually came face to face with a God who could not be ignored.

Bobby and Tommy tackle such diverse hot potatoes as dreary church buildings, worry, sex, diets, chocolate, the Devil, and trying to impress God. Nothing in the boys' collection of favourite thoughts, true stories, hymns, poems or prayers is profane, just truly unique.

It's not a book for the faint-hearted as there are as many twists, turns, challenges and surprises as there are in the Cannon & Ball stage act.

As you would expect from a pair who have devoted their whole lives to making people laugh, this book is filled with as much humour as can be squeezed into a limited volume. It's not surprising, then, that Bobby and Tommy want to use this gift of laughter, unique to humans, as a way of presenting the Good News of the gospel in an entertaining and yet thought-provoking way.

It's also a book of reflection, encouragement and hope. Both of the boys have faced their ups and downs, and the fame and fortune of showbiz doesn't isolate anyone from the difficulties of life. They both admit that they probably wouldn't have got through all the trials and traumas of past years without their faith. What they offer is a holy tonic and a spiritual refresher to men and women alike.

So, prepare to laugh, cry, think, take a step back, take a step forward, and re-examine where your own spirituality lies as you enter the unique world of *The Gospel According to Cannon & Ball*.

Chris Gidney
March 2007

Curtain Up

 I'm quite excited because I've been told I can start this book off all by myself, which is fantastic. Having had to put up with Bobby's interruptions on stage for the last 40 years, it's going to be a great relief. How much I can get away with before Bob comes bouncing on I've no idea, but I have already prayed 'O Lord, give me patience, and GIVE IT TO ME NOW!'

Don't Hang Around

 Hi, Tommy! I just thought I'd pop in and see if you need any help. By the way, St Peter sees a guy behind the Golden Gate of Heaven and says, 'Come in.'

'In a minute,' says the guy.

'You can come in right now,' says St Peter.

'In a minute!' says the guy, getting infuriated.

'What are you waiting for? Come on in now,' says St Peter.

'In a minute!' shouts back the guy.

'You do know you're dead, don't you?' says St Peter.

'I do,' says the guy. 'But can you please tell these cardiac arrest people!'

A Life of Laughter

 Thanks, Bobby! I knew it wouldn't be long before he popped up with a gag. He's always ready with a joke or three! Like me, we both love making people laugh, and we've spent our whole lives doing just that. We hope that as you read this book, you will have plenty of opportunities to laugh, and – as we will show you later – laughing is very good for you. We also hope that our thoughts will help you think about the spiritual side of life and the essential ingredients we have found important in order to live a life as full as was originally intended.

Ready for a Service?

 A young lad was visiting a church for the first time, checking all the announcements and posters along the walls.

When he came to a group of pictures of men in uniform, he asked a nearby usher, 'Who are all those men in the pictures?'

The usher replied, 'Why, those are our boys who died in the service.'

Dumbfounded, the youngster asked, 'Was that the morning service or the evening service?'

A Family Business

 Well, my real name is Tommy Derbyshire, but I'm called Cannon on stage because 'Derbyshire & Ball' doesn't seem to fit! I'm married to a beautiful woman called Hazel and I've got a full house of descendants. There's Kelly, Zoe and Luke, my children, three grandchildren and one great-grandchild. Oh yes, I've been working hard, you know!

What amazes me is what the kids have today. I would play soccer with a rolled-up newspaper, tied together with a piece of string until it all fell apart. My kids have got X-boxes, PlayStations, and MP3 players. I told them the other day that all I got for my birthday was an apple and an orange. 'What, a mobile phone and a computer?' they said!

It's so tempting to buy them everything they want and to do our best as parents to 'keep up with the Joneses', for fear of our children feeling second-class. However, I have to say that no amount of money or possessions can take the place of true parental love. A smile and a hug today can mean so much more than a new pair of trainers, and lasts a lot longer too!

Read the Label

 A schoolteacher watched her classroom of children while they drew. She would occasionally walk around to see each pupil's artwork. As she came to one little girl who was working diligently, she asked what the drawing was.

The girl replied, 'I'm drawing God.'

The teacher paused and said, 'But no one knows what God looks like.'

Without missing a beat, or looking up from her drawing, the girl replied, 'Well, they will do in a minute.'

Yes, I know, I love gags. I can't resist hearing them, discovering them, and using them. I do think laughter is God's greatest medicine. However, like all medicine it only works if it's used in the right way; if it isn't it becomes like drug abuse. Something that is intended for good health becomes destructive. I think there is a fine line here, particularly in comedy, but as the great Goon Harry Secombe once said, 'You can laugh at anything so long as it doesn't hurt anybody.'

4

Prayer Texting

Prayer can be pretty confusing. If God knows everything, why do we need to pray at all? I think I found part of the answer recently when I suddenly got a text from my grandson. I hadn't seen him for a while, but I'd not forgotten him. When his text came through it brought him nearer to my mind, and I sent a text back and started a conversation. Perhaps that's what prayer is like? When, amid our busy lives we decide to send God a quick prayer, we know he already cares about us, but it allows him to enter our lives again.

Why Did God Create Eve?

10 God worried that Adam would always be lost in the Garden because men hate to ask for directions.

9 God knew that Adam would one day need someone to hand him the TV remote. (Men don't want to see what's ON television, they want to see WHAT ELSE is on!)

8 God knew that Adam would never buy a new fig leaf when his seat wore out and would therefore need Eve to get one for him.

7 God knew that Adam would never make a doctor's appointment for himself.

6 God knew that Adam would never remember which night was dustbin night.

5 God knew that if the world was to be populated, men would never be able to handle childbearing.

4 As 'Keeper of the Garden', Adam would never remember where he put his tools.

3 The scripture account of Creation indicates Adam

needed someone to blame his troubles on when God caught him hiding in the garden.

2 As the Bible says, 'It is not good for man to be alone!'

1 When God finished the creation of Adam, he stepped back, scratched his head and said, 'I can do better than that.'

God Is Multilingual

 It's funny how odd we sometimes become when we talk to God. Perhaps we adopt a certain position; we bow, kneel or face one direction; sometimes we grip our head as if we have a headache or a nosebleed. Really, the only biblical description of physical prayer is in 1 Timothy 2, verse 8, which says we can pray, 'Lifting holy hands up to the Lord'. We don't need sophisticated words; we can just talk to God normally because he loves us just as we are.

Inside Out

 I know you won't believe it, but I was an ugly kid. I was that ugly when I was born that the hospital put me in an incubator with tinted windows. When I first came out, the midwife slapped my mother. We were very poor when we were kids too. I didn't even have a tin bath, mine was paper. My mother used to get my school uniform from the world-famous Army & Navy Stores, which was fine, but you try going to school dressed as a Japanese Army Frogman! Now I live in a posh place called Lytham St Anne's. Unfortunately, it's for old people and I'm the only one there with my own hips, and all the shop windows are bifocal. Humans are a very strange creation, and I'm just so grateful that God looks on the inside more than the outside.

Religion or Fact?

 I'm not religious. I don't think Christianity has anything to do with religion anyway. That word makes me think of old, out-of-date churches who are still living in the past, whereas my faith is a living, vibrant thing that makes sense for today. I understand that the word 'religion' in Latin actually refers to piety, but the word 'spiritual' comes from the French word *esprit* and refers to breath or breathing. It's a living thing, and every time I breathe in and out I feel I am connected to the One who makes my life worthwhile.

Love Is the Greatest

 I met my wife at the Stockton Fiesta Club. She was working as a bouncer there. That was nearly 40 years ago, and now she's hit an age that women hit and they become the wives you didn't marry. It's called the change of life. She's even started getting these hot flushes. Last Christmas it was freezing in Blackpool, and yet every one of the windows in my house was open.

'Is it hot in here or is it me?' she said.

You can always tell a woman is going through the change 'cos they get hot flushes, but also start wearing flannelette pyjamas! They also start to go on all sorts of strange diets. My wife is on a liquid diet at the moment. She liquidizes everything. Yesterday she drank three chickens and chocolate gateaux! The most important thing is that whatever she is like, I love her to bits, and I know she puts up with me because she loves me too. Love is a very powerful thing and overlooks our imperfections. 'Love is eternal. There are inspired messages, but they are temporary; there are gifts of speaking in strange tongues, but they will cease; there is knowledge, but it will pass.' So, in 1 Corinthians 13, verse 8, it says that love is here to stay.

The Dieter's Prayer

 Lord, my soul is ripped with riot,
Incited by my wicked diet.

'We are what we eat,' said a wise old man.
Lord, if that's true, I'm a garbage can.

I want to rise on Judgement Day, that's plain,
But at my present weight I'll need a crane.

So grant me strength that I may not fall
Into the clutches of cholesterol.

May my flesh with carrot curls be sated,
That my soul may be polyunsaturated.

And show me the light that I may bear witness
To the Government's Council on Physical Fitness.

Give me this day, my daily slice
But cut it thin and toast it twice.

I beg upon my dimpled knees,
Deliver me from those Smarties.

I can do it, Lord, if you'll show to me
The virtues of lettuce and celery.

And when my days of trial are done
And my war with malted milk is won,
Let me stand with the saints in heaven
In a shining robe, size thirty-seven!

God Speaks

Yes, it's a fact! God does actually talk to us. It says in 1 Kings 19, verse 12, 'After the earthquake there was a fire, but the Lord was not in the fire. And after the fire there was the soft whisper of a voice.' I think God today often speaks in a still small voice, so perhaps the problem is that we are so frequently surrounded by too much noise to be able to hear him properly. Try grabbing a coffee, sitting down with a piece of paper, and writing out six things that are important in your life at the moment. Read your list as if you are reading it to God, then spend some time in silence to see what God wants to say to you. It's amazing how we get fresh insight and understanding when we allow a small window for God in our busy day.

Family Matters

I've been married to Yvonne for over 30 years. I've got three kids, nine grandkids and two dogs. I've got one dog that is a cross between a pit bull and a St Bernard. If it bites your leg off, it runs for help. I'm so grateful for my family and I love having them around me. I'm also thankful that God has given me a heavenly family. As in all families, I may not get on with them all, but I thank God every day that he didn't ask me to live in isolation, but to share my spiritual journey with others.

Everything and Nothing

There was a time when Bobby and I were making so much money that we could buy anything we wanted. One summer in Torquay I was a bit bored, so I went out and bought a £40,000 boat. The problem was every time I went on it, I was seasick. We thought we had everything, several cars, chauffeurs, big houses abroad, but actually we had nothing. Nothing that really mattered. And none of the things I owned bought me real happiness. It was never enough. Never satisfying. I didn't know it at the time, but everything I have is only loaned to me. I can't take it with me because it belongs to God. He soon took it all away, and now we have none of the early trappings of fame. I have to say I'm a happier person without it.

My Friend

I wrote this poem when I was feeling very low, and through it I discovered that Jesus is a real friend.

Have you ever felt so lost
That you didn't know where to go?
Have you ever felt so lonely
On your own, wondering how you got so low?

Have you ever felt ashamed
Of the things you've done with the passing of time
Then you put your guilt away in little boxes
For no one to see like they were some sort of crime?

Have you ever felt you just need someone to talk to
Someone who will be there, who won't judge or
    criticize
Someone who will just love you for what you are
Not someone who is transparent and tells lies?

Have you ever wanted someone you could turn too
In your deepest troubles and need
Someone who will genuinely help you and love you
Without any ulterior motive, or greed?

Have you ever wanted someone who'll stand beside
    you
Whatever you're going through
Who will whisper in your ear
'I love you so much; I want to make everything
    brand new'?

Have you ever wanted someone
Who is with you every day
Someone you could trust and turn to
Someone who loves you so much, for you, he would
    give his life away?

Well, I know someone who loves you
Who wants to be with you till the end
So just open your heart and prepare to meet
Jesus, our friend.

Making Up

One day, at the height of our fame as Cannon & Ball, we fell out and stopped talking to each other for five years. It was such a desperate and sad time because we were at the top of our profession, yet too proud to even look at each other off stage. We even had dressing rooms on opposite sides of the stage. When I think back, it still brings tears to my eyes because of all the pain we endured. These days, I would have done things differently. No wonder there's a bit in the Bible about making up with your mate before coming before God. If you've recently fallen out with someone, ask God how you can heal that relationship. Even if it takes a very long time, and is one-sided, it will still be worth it because you will be free of the hurt that such a division can bring into your life. I'm so glad that one of the most important things that God has done in my life is to reconcile me with Bob.

The Opposite Sex

 I have recently been told that there is evidence that there will be no women in heaven because Revelation 8, verse 1, says: 'When the Lamb broke open the seventh seal, there was silence in heaven for about half an hour.' Ouch! That's Yvonne giving me a punch!

A Change of Heart

 It was one pantomime season in Bradford that Bobby suddenly came up to me and simply said my name. 'Tom'. Then he said that he had asked Jesus into his life. I was dumbstruck. He's not spoken to me for nearly five years and he comes out with a statement like that. I was ready to hit him. Then I decided that he was probably losing his marbles and I should leave it. I walked quickly away, but kept a close eye on him. Over the next few months I could see that whatever had happened to Bobby was for real. He had completely changed.

Caution: God at Work

 One summer season we were at the Britannia Pier in Great Yarmouth, and still had dressing rooms on the opposite side of the stage, but we were talking a bit better. One day I walked into Bobby's room and saw four guys sitting there all holding hands. Now to me, that wasn't a good sign! I shut the door quickly and walked away with a red face. I really thought that Bobby was going to 'come out'. Of course he was just praying with a pastor from the charity called Christians In Entertainment. Little did I know that they were praying for me! Even though I had no idea about God and faith, I could see that something unique was happening. Even people who don't know God can sense him when he's at work.

A Christian Hamburger

This new-found faith was something I was really keen to be a part of. It was as if someone had been down to the shops and got a free packet of biscuits with a jar of coffee and not told me. I felt pretty left out and was determined to try my best to make it happen. The first thing I did was buy a gold chain with a cross on it to go around my neck. Then I bought some nice religious poems and hung them on my dressing room wall. But as someone once said, 'Going to church doesn't make you a Christian any more than going to McDonald's makes you a hamburger!' In other words, it isn't going to church that gives you faith, or reading the right books, nor is it believing in God. Satan believes in God. It's having a personal one-to-one relationship that makes you a Christian. I could see that this is what Bobby had, but I didn't know how to get it for myself. However, when we seek God, he always helps us find him.

Musical Chairs

My experiences of church were not good. When my mother took me as a child, it was like entering a library. It was silent apart from a forlorn organ playing something very

GO OVER AND STOP THOSE TWO KIDS MAKING NOISE IN CHURCH IMMEDIATELY... WE DON'T WANT THEM GROWING UP TO BE SOME KIND OF COMEDIANS...

solemn, and if I even so much as coughed I would get a dozen steely glares across the pews and my mother would be trying to strangle me. No one could sit in someone else's pew and we sat in the same seat every single Sunday. Thank goodness most churches are not like that any more. However, sitting in the same place every week still seems to happen. I would love to play that party game where everyone has to move seats in church when the music stops. It would just be a reminder that God doesn't want us to go stagnant, but is eager for us to keep moving on in our spiritual lives.

Shine a Light

Why is it that when I go to so many churches that the sound and lighting system is so old and inadequate that I can neither be seen or heard? I can understand the fear of turning a church from a place of worship into a theatre, but surely the Good News is worth the best platform we have? If the Bible says we should be like a light, then let's make it bright enough to hear what God is saying.

Rockin' Rolling Faith

It was when I went to a church in Wales that Bobby had invited me to that all my preconceptions of churches being cold, and for the over-seventies, was blown away. It was brightly lit, with a rock'n'roll band, singers, Smarties for the kids, and a minister who seemed passionate about what he was saying. I even got hugged and kissed on the cheek by a huge Welshman as I walked in! I was worried for a bit because I had recently seen Bobby sitting in his dressing rooms holding hands with these other blokes! However, as I looked around this bright and friendly church I was amazed at the rock'n'roll band that started up and the animated choir. I thought that if this was one way to praise the Lord, then surely this was a great way to do it. It was something that seemed so relevant to today rather than being stuck in the past. There's nothing wrong with a church full of older people, but what happens when they all pass on? Someone will buy the church and turn it into a disco. Some churches are so miserable, and it doesn't help if you have to walk through a graveyard to get to the front door. I'd rather see church as a living resource bringing God into the community, but that means we have to work hard to make it an interesting and exciting place to be. How can you introduce a little taste of heaven into your church?

Opening the Door

Although I enjoyed the service I looked at my watch and thought to myself that I would be out of there soon, and on to a game of golf. It was the pastor, Ray, who

then said, 'I'm sure there are some people out there who would like to know more about God and perhaps let him into their life.' He asked everyone to close their eyes to pray, but to put up their hands if they wanted to ask God to meet them in a new and special way. I was pretty sceptical, but while thinking through all the pros and cons it was as if my hand went up by itself. I caught my wife's eyes, which clearly said, 'What on earth are you doing?' The next time I looked across, she had her hand up too. Only you ladies can change your minds in two seconds! In front of a packed church I went forward that morning, not a little embarrassed, except that my desire to know God properly was more important to me than what other people thought. It was the best thing I ever did.

Whatever Next?

After I had asked God to have a bigger say in my life, I wondered what was going to happen next. I almost expected a knock at the door and for Jesus to walk in. At first I felt a bit disappointed that something more dramatic hadn't occurred. There were no flashing lights or thunderbolts or anything except that I felt different, but couldn't explain how or why. Then I discovered the art of talking to God. 'Thanks' was the first thing I said. I realized that I was now away from the razzmatazz of that church and it was now just 'Him' and me. It was a lovely thought, and I knew that a new journey in my life had just begun.

The Clockmaker

It's strange when we spend so much time trying different things to sort out our lives when the answer is so obvious. If a clock breaks down, I could take it to the butcher, the baker or the candlestick maker, but none of them would be able to fix it. No, I take my broken clock to the clock-maker. He knows intimately how all the complex cogs and wheels and hands work because he is the one who crafted it. He is the only one who really knows how to repair my clock to as good as new. I don't need to look for other solutions. I can simply take myself back to God.

A Working Faith

I was playing around with my youngest grandson, when he was 16, when he complained that his neck hurt. Just a few weeks later, his Mum phoned me to say that a lump on his neck had been diagnosed as cancerous. As you can imagine, I was devastated. I jumped in my car straight away and drove several hundred miles to see him, praying all the way. On that long journey, as I chatted away, I felt as if God was putting an arm around my shoulder and saying that it was going to be all right. When I arrived at his house the atmosphere was terrible, and as I looked at my grandson I could see that he was angry. *Very* angry. I told him I had been praying for him all the way in the car, and that I knew that he would be carrying me in my coffin before I carried him. He asked me how I knew all that, and I said it was because I had chatted to the 'Boss'. Today, several worrying months later, he is clear. I have to tell you that God helped me and my family through that awful time. If I hadn't had God beside me, I really don't know what I would have done. I can turn to my friends, but it's just not the same as leaning on a God who understands and cares for me better than anyone.

What a Difference

Having God in my life has completely changed everything and it would take a whole book just to explain the differences, but – unlike before – I look forward to going home when I've been away; knowing God has made my marriage much better and increased my love and understanding for my children and grandchildren. Bobby has become my best friend in the whole world, and there is nothing I wouldn't do for him. Having God in my life hasn't stopped the problems, but it means I have someone who will walk through life with me every step of the way. God has given me so much, I just spend each and every day thanking him.

Tripping Over Myself

Me and Tommy slogged around the clubs for three years before we got what they call 'an overnight success'! I was a keen family man at the time, but this huge rise to fame completely changed my life. From being a family that would turn off the lights and hide from the rent man, we were able to buy several houses which were as big as we liked. The sad thing was that because of my ego problem, which was created by sudden stardom, I pushed my family to one side. No wonder God says that the thing he hates more than anything else, is pride. James 4, verse 6, says, 'God resists the proud.' No wonder it felt like God was a million miles away at that time. I don't think this verse means it's wrong to take pride in your work, or your family or what you have achieved, it's when we think we are the most important people on the earth that we can run into serious problems. Anyone who thinks they've got it all sorted out probably hasn't.

Even for Christians, it's when we think we know all the answers that we can find God having to show us that we actually know very little.

Anchors Away

 One year, in the early days of fame and success, I was away for 48 weeks. I didn't see my wife and kids for that long because I was continuously on tour. I had my own entourage whose job it was to push me from car to stage to hotel room, and back to the car again. Eventually the monotony and lack of any anchor in my life caused me to turn to drink. Not just the odd drink here and there, but a bottle and a half of whisky every day. Every single day. It got so bad that in London one night after the show I went to a nightclub, got completely blotto, and ended up lying in a back-street in a drunken stupor, where it was the job of my bodyguard to find me before the press found out. In those days, that's the sort of thing that could kill a career. Looking back now, I can see how important it is to have an anchor in our lives. I love that children's hymn written by Priscilla Jane Owens that goes:

> We have an anchor that keeps the soul.
> Steadfast and sure while the billows roll.
> Fastened to the Rock which cannot move.
> Grounded firm and deep in the Saviour's love.

I just wish I'd paid more attention at Sunday school!

Big Brother

People ask us why we are not on the telly so much these days, and the answer is we can't cook and we're no good at gardening! My wife watches *Big Brother*, and I think she's addicted to it. I can't understand it 'cos she even watches it when they're all asleep! That programme drives me mad, but I'm grateful that God keeps an eye on us all the time. It makes me feel safe and secure knowing that my real Big Brother watches over me.

Public Faith

Jesus was born round the back of a pub. He was used to talking with the man on the street. He spent a lot of time in the equivalent of the pub, so much so that he was accused of being a glutton and a drunkard. He even had lunch with a tax collector! Jesus loved engaging with people, and I bet he was a good listener too. He is still in the business of meeting with people, and he wants to meet you today.

Words, Words, Words

 I used to carry round with me the greatest weapon known to mankind and I used it regularly: my tongue. I was very good at using my words to cut people into little pieces. I think that the biggest lie we heard at school was: 'Sticks and stones will break my bones, but words will never hurt me.'

It's very easy to hurt the ones we love by not being careful in what we say. Every time we open our mouths, all that should come out is love.

It's interesting that the Bible puts gossip at the top of the hit list as something that can be very destructive, but God used his words to create the world when he started the whole thing in Genesis by saying:

Let there be light, and there was light.

Let's use our words wisely too.

In James 3, verse 3–6, it says, 'We put a bit into the mouth of a horse to make it obey us, and we are able to make it go where we want. Or think of a ship: big as it is and driven by such strong winds, it can be steered by a very small rudder, and it goes wherever the pilot wants it to go. So it is with the tongue: small as it is, it can boast about great things. Just think how large a forest can be set on fire by a tiny flame!'

What a Wonderful World

 I do admire atheists because they have much more faith than I do. To have the ability to look at the incredible Creation all around us, the rolling seas, the amazing animals, the beautiful flowers, and then be able to say that it was all a big mistake must take an incredible amount of faith. Much more than I have. Apart from Creation, seeing the birth of a baby is the most incredible thing. Understanding how the human body is so wonderfully made is astonishing, and trying to understand how the human brain works leaves me speechless.

A Weight off My Mind

 At one time I was messing around with a lot of women, and I mean a *lot*! I didn't realize it then, but everything we do in life we pick it up and carry. It's only when we come to God and hand over all those things that we have lugged around that we finally become free. Till then, we are bound down by the weight of life which becomes heavier and heavier until it's almost too heavy to cope with any more. We can push things that we are ashamed of to the back of our minds, but every now and again they pop forward, and we try to push them back again. Nowadays I don't need to be bothered with all of that. I just pull them out and give them to God. That's why his son Jesus Christ died, so that we can have freedom and a very abundant life.

God Is What?

 We are made of flesh and bone. A car is made of steel. A table is made of wood. If you ask the Bible what God is made of, you'll find John 1, verse 8, gives quite an unexpected reply. 'God is Love' says the King James version. That seems to be the perfect answer to me. God is a huge being full of more love that I can ever imagine.

Getting It All

I attacked a vicar. Not with my fists, but with my words. I wanted to destroy his argument that God even existed. I was never a great lover of vicars but, looking back, I think it was more out of a fear that if he was proved right, and that there was a God, then I would have to change my lifestyle, something I really didn't want to do.

Without this vicar even having to say a word, I was angry at him coming to see me as if he was better than I was. I didn't think I had done anything wrong, and I certainly hadn't raped or killed anybody, so I thought I was going to heaven anyway. What I hadn't realized was that I couldn't go to heaven unless I knew God personally. He doesn't want to wait until we're dead, because he wants to know us now.

'I'm better than you,' I said. 'I've got a big Rolls-Royce, a yacht, more money than I can spend, and two girls waiting for me back at my hotel. I've got a huge house, and you live in a place that the church gives you, so is God blessing me or you? God's blessing me, isn't he, because you've got nothing?'

'I've got peace,' was all he said as he left, and that really annoyed me. I was climbing the wall, because it was true. He had something I didn't have. I had everything material in the world I could have, but I didn't have what this simple vicar had. Although I was frustrated with him, something in me was strangely drawn to him too, because I could see that something important was missing in my life.

Get Thee to a Nunnery

'Max, I want to get to know God, but I'm frightened,' I said, as we sat in his little front room at the vicarage.

'Why's that?' he asked very patiently.

'Because I don't want to be like those Christians I've seen with long faces and hundred-pound Bibles under their arms.'

He laughed.

'Nor do I want to become a monk or anything, or wear open-toed sandals. Most of all, I don't want to be laughed at.'

The idea of tough Bobby Ball, top of the profession, appearing on television with Tommy every week, becoming part of the God-squad, made me shiver to even think about it. I knew everyone would laugh. If not openly, then certainly behind my back. I couldn't cope with that. I also told Max that I didn't think I could change my lifestyle. I knew I couldn't, in my own strength, stop doing the things I hated.

'Why not let God worry about all that?' Max asked.

I wanted to know God so badly that I decided there and then to do just that, and it was my first lesson in letting go and handing things over to God.

Delete and Start Again

I understand Bobby's desperation to be able to blot out the past and start again. This poem seems to say it all in a very humorous way:

Don't you wish when life is bad
and things just don't compute,
That all we really had to do
was stop and hit reboot?

Things would all turn out OK,
life could be so sweet,
If we had those special keys
ctrl-and alt-delete

Your boss is mad, your bills not paid
your wife, well she's just mute.
Just stop and hit those wonderful keys
that make it all reboot.

You'd like to have another job,
you fear living in the street?
You solve it all and start anew
with ctrl and alt delete.

New Oil

I always thought God's name was Harold. That's because at school we always prayed, 'Harold be thy name!'

When Max the vicar offered to pray with me it was the first time I had ever done so. I was very nervous and felt a bit stupid. What I wanted most of all was a chance to get rid of my past and start again. I realized that this was a chance to do just that.

'Repeat the words after me,' he explained. 'But when you speak, don't speak to me, speak to God because he's listening.'

I got three lines in before I started sobbing. I felt God come into me from the top of my head all the way through my body. I felt washed and clean and forgiven and brand-new. Most of all I felt loved. I cried for three days afterwards with the mixture of relief and freedom that I felt. I still pray every day and ask God to give me a spiritual MOT and the occasional divine oil change because there's nothing like it for revitalizing my spiritual engine.

Just Ask

No sooner had I tucked up my son Luke in his bed for the night than he was shouting down the stairs:

'Dad, please can I have a glass of water?'

'No, you've already had enough to drink,' I called back, 'Now you must go to sleep.'

A few minutes passed then:

'Dad. Please can I have a glass of water?'

'No!' I said firmly. 'It's sleep time now.'

A few more minutes went by and then:

'Dad. *Please*, please can I have a glass of water?'

I was getting cross.

'No, Luke! If you ask me once more, I shall have to come upstairs and give you a smack!'

'OK,' came the reply. 'But when you come upstairs to give me a smack, can you please bring me a glass of water?'

This is a lovely story all about persistence, and I'm glad that we can ask God as many times as we like about the things we need and he will never get fed up with us asking. What a wonderful thought.

Thank You, Lord

Not long after I let God into my life, this song just flowed into my mind one day and I've often sung it on stage as part of our Gospel Show. The words are still close to my heart:

I want to thank you, Lord
'Cos you kissed away my rain
Took away all my pain
You died on the cross for me
And all the pain you went through
So I could start my life anew
I get on my knees to you
And I thank you, Lord.

A Big Yawn

One thing I was worried about was that when I became a Christian my life would become very dull. I could see that Christians had a peace about them that I wanted, but I thought they were very boring. I thought I had the lifestyle that was exciting, but I have to say that there is nothing more exciting than giving your life to God. Within weeks of asking God to become my guide, he was taking me to places and giving me experiences that I had never known before.

Misunderstood Man

 I was in a church one day when the notices were being read out, and the solemn-looking guy at the front spoke with a completely straight face. 'Please would the congregation be aware that the notice on the collection box at the back of the church which reads, "for the sick" is not to be taken literally!' I had to stop myself from laughing out loud, but it did remind me how we sometimes mis-understand what God really says to us. It's important to think carefully about what the Bible and other Christians say as taking it literally isn't always what is meant. Several times the Bible says we should weigh things up, or test things out, before we accept them.

Teamwork

When I gave my life to God, the first thing I did was to go home and tell Yvonne I was sorry for the way in which I had treated her. She said she would try to forgive me, but when six months later Yvonne also gave her life to God, our past was really healed. It was the most wonderful thing that could have happened because now we are a real team. Together, we can tell people about how good God has been and what a change he has made to our lives. I think a partnership of husband and wife is a vital thing and something to be worked on and cherished as much as possible.

Sat Nav

It's amazing when I consider the fact that God has a plan for every single person. I don't think it's the sort of plan that says what biscuits you should eat next or which bus to catch. I imagine that God's plan is more like a special destination that he knows will be perfect for us, and he wants to show us the best way to get there. As with all maps, there are often many different routes we can take, perhaps a slow route via the 'B' roads or a faster one on a motorway. This is the flexibility that God gives us, as we make our way through life, one step at a time; it doesn't always matter how I got there so long as I arrive safely and in one piece. I've got a satellite navigation system in my car, and anyone who has got one knows what a wonderful help they are these days. It tells me when to turn left and when to turn right, and when I make a mistake, often because I'm not listening properly, it gets me back on track pretty soon. I'm so grateful for a heavenly and personal navigation system God has placed within me called the Holy Spirit.

A Real Getaway

We seem to plan everything these days, particularly holidays. My wife will go down to the travel agents and come back with a huge range of brochures standing two-foot high, but we still always end up going to Tenerife! Then when we get to the airport the first thing anyone sees, if they are afraid of flying, is the word 'Terminal'! We try to speak the language while all the locals laugh, stay in a tiny room with a view of the car park, get sunburned, and end up with a bad case of the trots. When we get back our friends ask if we've had a good time?

'Oh yes!' we lie. 'We're going back again next year!'

I think it's better to leave God to do most of the planning for our life's journey. Imagine you are on the highway of life, and on either side are the worldly travel agents advertising their wares: Greed Getaways; Anger Adventures and Lust Locations. You try all these and, in so doing, fill up your suitcase with so much junk you can hardly carry it. Each holiday, no matter how good it sounds, just doesn't seem to bring the satisfaction that you were promised. Then one day you see a little shop at the end of the road called Heavenly Holidays.

'Welcome,' says the friendly voice as you step inside to take a peak at what's on offer. 'It's really good to see you. I've been waiting for you.'

'What's heaven like?' you ask.

'It's fantastic,' comes the excited response. 'In fact, it's that good, no one ever comes back.'

'Have you been?'

'Yes.'

'So why have you come back then?'

'Because this is my father's business,' the shopkeeper says.

'How much is it to go?'

'It's free. I've bought you a ticket.'

'How much did that cost?'

'This much,' came the reply as he held out his hands to reveal the nailprints in them.

'What's the accommodation like?'

'It's mansions.'

'I really want to go.'

'That's good, but read the brochure first,' and he hands over a Bible.

'I'm sorry for all the places I shouldn't have gone,' you say.

With that, you're handed a brand-new passport stamped with the word 'forgiven'. Then the shopkeeper gently takes the old battered suitcase and empties all the rubbish out of it. It feels so much lighter now. Despite worrying about an empty suitcase, you are assured that from now on you won't need anything as it will all be provided.

You leave the shop and arrive at the airport only to see that there is pandemonium at the Heavenly Holidays check-in. Everyone is trying to get through. Some are fighting, some are arguing, some are trying to bribe, and some are simply begging. You just walk up to the clerk at the counter who takes one look at your new passport and says,

'Oh, so you've met Jesus. Please go straight through.'

Passing the Duty Free you suddenly realize that it really is free! After filling up your empty suitcase with all manner of God's gifts, you are amazed at how light it still feels.

I'm in the departure lounge of life and I've got a new passport. Have you got yours?

Free Membership

Christianity isn't some private club. Yet how often do we sit there in our four walls talking about how nice the flowers look or whether we've heard the latest gossip about Mrs Moonstone's hernia. Sometimes I would like to shut all the churches for a month and encourage all the churchgoers to go down to the pub instead. There we can talk to real people about the Good News of the gospel. That's what Jesus did. He was found more often talking about spiritual things outside the church than inside it, and was not restricted by buildings and schedules. It would be nice if sometimes we could follow his example.

Get in Touch

It's so easy to get in touch with God, even if – like me – you never really knew him in the first place, whether you've turned your back on him and wandered off on your own, or whether you've known him for the whole of your life. Here's a simple prayer that I use, not just for the once, but on a daily basis:

Dear God,
I come to you as a sinner and I know that I've done wrong and I ask you to forgive me. I believe that Jesus Christ died on the cross so that I could be free. Father, please take away my pain, my hurt and my guilt, and fill me with your Spirit. I accept your presence in my life and the healing you have to offer me. In Jesus' name. Amen.

Saying Sorry

It was Elton John who penned the song 'Sorry seems to be the hardest word'. This is a prayer that I find helpful to get me back on track once in a while:

Dear Heavenly Father,
We lower our heads before you and we confess that we have too often forgotten that we are yours. Sometimes we carry on our lives as if there were no God and we fall short of being a credible witness to you. For these things we ask your forgiveness and we also ask for your strength. Give us clear minds and open hearts so we may witness to you in our world. Remind us to be who you would have us to be regardless of what we are doing or who we are with.

Hold us to you and build our relationship with you and with those you have given us on earth.

Trouble at Mill

 It always amazes me how often we struggle along on our own without asking for God's help. You may have trouble in your marriage, your family, your work, and your finances. That's normal because we don't live in a perfect world. We have to expect that things will go wrong. The difference is that when you have God in your life, you don't have to manage it alone. Talk to him now about your worries and your problems. He understands, he cares, he wants to listen, and to help too. And, believe me, there's no one better!

Choices

 Liza Minnelli once said that 'Religion is for people who are afraid to go to hell, and faith is for people who have already been there.' I like that thought as, to me, religion always seems to be man-made, whereas faith is heaven-sent. I know which one I prefer.

How to Get a Bull's-eye

I'm told that in golf if you hit the ball and it goes off course and is in danger of hitting someone, you are supposed to shout 'Fore!' as loud as you can. In Medieval times, if the arrow missed the target, you had to shout 'Sinner'. This is where we get our biblical word from, and although it sounds a bit dated, it explains our spiritual situation very well. No matter how hard we try, we shall never be able to hit the target. In Romans 3, verse 23, it says, 'For we have all fallen short of the glory of God . . .' With God at our side, however, he will help us get a bull's-eye every time.

Say That Again?

We have an ongoing joke that whenever Chris from 'Christians in Entertainment' comes to see me and Bobby he does the same Bible Study on the loaves and two fishes every time, and we always complain that he has nothing new to deliver. (A bit like his stage act!) He doesn't really, but we like to wind him up. It's actually a reminder that the Bible repeats itself quite often, probably because we are so slow at listening and God feels like he needs to say it over and over so we don't miss out. A good example is when it says 'Do not worry' in some form or other 366 times throughout the Bible. That's because God knows I need to hear those words each and every day, and there's even one left over for leap year! Could you say that again please, God?

Are You Listening, God?

A man was walking through a forest pondering life. He walked, pondered, walked, and pondered. He felt very close to nature and even close to God. He felt so close to God that he felt if he spoke, God would listen.

So he asked, 'God, are you listening?'

And God replied, 'Yes, my son, I am here.'

The man stopped and pondered some more.

He looked towards the sky and said, 'God, what is a million years to you?'

God replied, 'Well, my son, a second to me is like a million years to you.'

So the man continued to walk and to ponder . . . walk and ponder . . .

Then he looked to the sky again and said, 'God, what is a million pounds to you?'

And God replied, 'My son, my son . . . a penny to me is like a million pounds to you. It means almost nothing to me. It does not even have a value, it is so little.'

The man looked down, pondered a bit, and then looked up to the sky and said, 'God, can I have a million pounds?'

And God replied, 'In a second.'

A New Manager

A newspaper article once said that I had become a Christian in order to further my career. In actual fact they were right, it was the best career move I ever made! I no longer have to rely just on agents because I have the best manager in the world now! He knows what is best for me, he knows what is right for me, and he knows how to use the gifts and talents he has invested in me in the best way possible. How can we lose?

Loud and Clear

 Jesus used the language of his day to talk to people. His parables were all based on situations, events and feelings that the people around him were familiar with. We must do the same today. If we put notices like 'Jesus saves' outside our churches, those passing may think it's talking about Clubcard points! A notice I recently read outside a church said the speaker for next Sunday will be hanging on the notice board in the foyer! Let's be straightforward and clear in what we say about our faith, because that's really the best way to be understood.

The Wrong Heroes

 It's so important not to live our faith through other Christians. There was a preacher I used to love listening to. He had great authority, was a great communicator, and I always left the service feeling spiritually high. One day I was astounded when I heard that he had been having huge personal problems and had left the ministry. For a while this news shocked me so much that I was left numb and confused. Then it dawned on me that I had relied too heavily on one person to lead me to God, and not put enough effort into building that relationship directly. Let's make sure we use the opportunity to talk to God directly rather than expecting someone else to act as a go-between.

Forget It

Worry is the darkroom in which negatives can develop.

Chimney Prayers

There can't have been many subjects more written about than the mystery of prayer. Some people see prayer like the BBC television programme *Jim'll Fix It* where you send in a request and, if you are lucky, it gets pulled out of the postbag and gets sorted. Others think that it's like Santa's Christmas list sent up the chimney every year, that if they ask for enough things, something is bound to be granted. Some imagine prayer is like the National Lottery, 'If I keep putting my pound in, at least I'm bound to get something back soon.' I can just imagine people praying with their fingers crossed just like the Lottery Logo! No, for me, prayer is simply a way of talking to my heavenly Father, and there's nothing God loves more than a good chat with the ones he loves!

Nun Left

 A nun was taking a shower one day and she heard the doorbell ring, so she yelled 'Who is it?'

And the person ringing the doorbell yelled, 'I'm the blind man.'

So the nun got out of the shower and wrapped her hair in a towel. She didn't bother putting a towel around herself because the person behind the door was blind.

She opened the door and said, 'What do you want?', and the man said, 'I'm here to check your blinds.'

Mobile Prayers

 I'm told that text messages passed 4 billion a month recently. We are a world that sees communication as important, and communication with heaven is vital too. So how many prayers do we send up in a month? Well, I believe there are currently just over 2 billion Christians in the world today, and if each of those was to pray twice a day, that would mean God is handling around 120 billion prayers a month. What a good job God has big ears!

Today's the Day

When I was 15 years old I discovered real music. Chuck Berry, Jerry Lee Lewis and Little Richard were my heroes. I'm not knocking the kids' music of today, but you can't whistle a rap! It was when I heard a bloke whistling and singing along at the welding firm that I worked at in Oldham that I met Tommy. We decided to form a double-act and I suppose the rest is history. The odd thing is that we were convinced we would be a musical act, but it's funny how the things we plan don't always turn out the way we expect, but that's why life is so exciting. I'd hate the thought of going to a psychic or palm reader, because I'd much rather face each day as it comes.

Togetherness

It's amazing when you think that 34,000 separate Christian groups have been identified in the world, and over half of them are independent churches that are not interested in linking with the big denominations. I often think it's a shame that Christians don't work together more often. It must be very confusing when someone who has no idea about our church life sees so many different denominations, and must come to the conclusion that none of them agree with each other. In church one week a respected lady came forward and said that while she had been praying with some friends God had given her a very encouraging picture. This was of a maypole with hundreds of coloured ribbons hanging down from the centre. Many people came forward to grasp these ribbons and dance. As they danced, the ribbons became entwined around each other and beautiful patterns of colour were formed. She felt this represented the many denominations and churches that were being urged to find a way to work as one.

God's Voice Mail

 We have all learned to live with voice mail as a necessary part of modern life. But you may have wondered, 'What if God decided to install voice mail?' Imagine praying and hearing this:

Thank you for calling My Father's House.
Please select one of the following options:

Press 1 for request
Press 2 for thanksgiving
Press 3 for complaints
Press 4 for all other inquiries
Thank you.'

If you would like to speak to Gabriel, press 1 now
If you would like to speak to Michael, press 2 now
For a directory of other angels, press 3 now
If you would like to hear King David sing a Psalm while you're holding, press 4 now
Thank you.'

All the angels are busy helping other customers with their enquiries. Please stay on the line. Your call is in a queue and will be answered as soon as possible. You are 3,700,678th in the queue.

When you eventually get through . . .

This office is closed for the weekend. Please call again on Monday after 9.00 a.m.

Big Ben

 Everywhere I look I am reminded of God's presence. Seeing a beautiful view, enjoying a flower's fragrance, marvelling at the power of the sea. Sometimes we are reminded of God and don't even realize it, like when I was in London a few weeks ago and heard the chimes of Big Ben once again. Apparently, this famous London landmark has a tune, which first sounded on 31 May 1859, and is called the 'Westminster Quarter', and is a variation on a theme in Handel's *Messiah*. Hallelujah!

The Pain

Perhaps sometimes we fall into the trap of making Jesus' death on a cross a bit too romantic. When I went to the Holy Land and they explained just what happened, it brought home to me the pain that Jesus must have gone through. This is a poem I wrote that reflects the reality of that suffering:

Feel the pain as the nails ripped through the flesh
Wear the crown of thorns, making the pain even
    worse not less
Hear the jeers and insults fall on your ears like
    drops of acid rain
Feel the pain of being deserted and tell me what is
    there to gain.

Feel the pain of splinters as they dig deep into your
    back
Feel the pain as you feel deserted and your mind is
    about to crack
Hear the hurt of hate and jeers and you look down
    upon the crowd
You try to tell them you love them, but the hate is
    too loud

You look at the sign above your head it simply says
    'King of the Jews'
You feel the pain because you came to save and
    never to abuse
Feel the pain because they don't understand that
    you are the great I am
Now they have nailed you to a cross because they
    don't believe that you are the creator of man.

Now I am sat here two thousand years later and I
   feel the pain of shame
It hurts me to think about what we did and the
   magnitude of your pain
So I am sorry, Jesus, that you had to feel the pain
   and that you had to die for me
But without your pain and without your death I
   would never have been free.

Thank you, Jesus.

Deal or No Deal?

 I'm sometimes asked to explain the cross
and why Jesus had to die. The easiest way I
understand this is that we live in an ordered
world where most rules are there for our
protection. If I drive through a red traffic light, I can
expect that I will get fined, have points put on my
licence, or even be sent to prison. At worst I may injure
or kill some innocent person in the process of breaking
the law and have to pay an even higher penalty. In the
same way God created the world, with rules from the
sun rising and setting to the best way to live our lives.
The problem was when humanity decided to turn its
back on God, the rules were broken, and a penalty
became due. The Bible says that this penalty is eternal
separation from God. In other words, death. The good
news is that because God loves us so much, he decided
he would pay the penalty that was due by Christ dying
on the cross. Christ died instead of me, and for me. My
fine has been paid, I've been set free, and instead of
facing eternal death I can enjoy eternal life with God.

Open the Box

The key about what Tommy has just said is that it's quite important to realize that you must actually accept the offer! If I'm in prison and someone comes along and offers to pay my fine and let me go, it won't happen unless I agree, take the money, pay the fine, and see the prison door open. Don't be stuck in jail when you could be enjoying life at its fullest.

No Laughing Matter

Did you know that comedians have the lowest divorce rate in showbiz? This is according to the latest research, which suggests that the ability to laugh and make others laugh must be a godsend for relationships. So, try turning to your loved one today and saying, 'I've just bought a microwave bed. It means I can get seven hours' sleep in three and a half minutes!'

BOBBY AND TOMMY ARE QUITE RIGHT ABOUT COMICS HAVING A LOW DIVORCE RATE... VERY HARD TO DO MOTHER-IN-LAW JOKES IF YOU NO LONGER HAVE A MOTHER-IN-LAW.

Slow Down, You Move Too Fast

 These two slugs decided to go on a race, so they set off and eventually turned round a corner to find themselves behind two snails. 'Oh no,' they said, 'Caravans!' Do you ever get impatient when things aren't going as fast as you would like? I do! But I have to remind myself sometimes that it's good to slow down and take in the scenery.

God's Boxes

 I was recently sent this lovely poem. The writer is anonymous, but is obviously in touch with one of our greatest problems, being unable to let go:

I have in my hands two boxes,
Which God gave me to hold.
He said, 'Put all your sorrows in the black box,
And all your joys in the gold.'

I heeded His words, and in the two boxes,
Both my joys and sorrows I stored,
But though the gold became heavier each day,
The black was as light as before.

With curiosity, I opened the black,
I wanted to find out why,
And I saw, in the base of the box, a hole,
Which my sorrows had fallen out by.

I showed the hole to God, and mused,
'I wonder where my sorrows could be!'
He smiled a gentle smile and said,
'My child, they're all here with me.'

I asked God, why he gave me the boxes,
Why the gold and the black with the hole?
'My child, the gold is for you to count your blessings,
The black is for you to let go.'

Don't Give Up

There's a very famous hairpin bend on a very long and steep hill near where I live in Yorkshire. Just a few weeks ago I turned the sharp corner as carefully as usual and I was glad that I did because I could easily have run over the two cyclists who were painstakingly making their way up the hill. I was so surprised to see them in all their cycling gear and noticed the vigour their bodies showed with each push of the pedal. I glanced at them again in my rear view mirror as I drove away and felt proud of what they were doing to reach the top of the hill. It occurred to me that their perseverance and determination was producing fitness and strength, and thought about those verses in the Bible that say '. . . suffering produces perseverance; perseverance, character; and character, hope' (Romans 5, verses 3–4).

Spiritual Fitness

I'm a great believer in being fit. I have to be in my job. Our recent pantomime season is a good example of this – I had to fall off a brick wall on stage six times at each performance. I think that makes it nearly 300 times in all, and that was for just one sketch! I try and get down to the gym at least once or twice a week and feel all the better for it. I suppose it is the same spiritually. We

spend so much time looking after our bodies with special diets, exercise, vitamin supplements and the rest, it's important we give the same attention to our spiritual fitness too.

V – For Victory

 According to a story, when the French bow-men captured English archers, they chopped off their first and second fingers, which were needed to draw the bow. The prisoners, now harmless, were then freed. The English knew what would happen to them if they were captured. So before battle, they enjoyed taunting the French lines by sticking two fingers up at them. It's funny how many things we take for granted have a history behind them. The sign of the cross, although used as a Christian symbol, is actually an instrument of torture and death. We'd never wear a gold electric chair around our necks, would we?

Spiritual Takeaways

Being away from home often means I eat all the wrong things. It's easier to pop into a McDonald's on the M1 or gulp down a late-night curry after a gig. The other tendency is to order a takeaway for my hotel room, but I'm always pleased when I can get back home to some really good food and home cooking. I think this idea works on a spiritual basis too. I can get a spiritual snack when I take a quick glance at my Bible, I can have a better meal perhaps in a home group, and then a full blown 'meat 'n' two veg' at church on a Sunday. All of these are good, so long as I don't rely just on a spiritual takeaway to keep me going.

Clutter Flutter

I'm amazed at the upsurge of storage facilities that have recently popped up all over the country. I wonder if we are becoming a nation of hoarders, even of things we don't really want or use any more. Do we rely too much on our possessions for security? A cluttered house is always a dangerous place to live. Falling over things and having nowhere to sit doesn't make for a restful way of life. Perhaps we should all take a look at what we have and start to de-clutter our lives. If we can give some of this to a local charity shop, then not only will it free us up, but benefit someone else as well.

Who Would?

This song came to me when I was thinking that, despite everything, Jesus has an enormous amount of love for us:

Would you be persecuted for the sake of me?
Would you be laughed at and ridiculed for the
    entire world to see?
Would you have the patience to try to make me
    understand
When all the time you could see that my soul was
    like shifting sand?

Would you still love me when all I caused you was
    hurt and pain?
Would you still love me when there was only loss
    and no gain?
Would you still love me if I kept turning my face
    away?
Would you keep loving me day after day after day?

Would you lay your life down for me and never
    count the cost?
Would you hold my hand, even though I was walk-
    ing with the lost?
Would you hold on to me and love me even though
    I was covered in sin?
Would you have enough love in your heart to help
    me begin again?

Would you love me enough to suffer agony, pain
    and humiliation?
Would you love me enough to be nailed to a cross
    for my salvation?
Would you love me enough to want the old me to
    be new?

Would you love me enough to want me to spend
eternity with you?
No?
Jesus does.

Talk, Talk

 Apparently, teenagers use an average of 22 words to communicate everything. As a father with a teenage son, I can confirm that! I just love it when my older kids call me for a chat, but as parents we've all been through those times when it seems your kids just phone you because they want something. Usually money! Isn't that so annoying? Imagine what it's like for our heavenly father, then, when we pray only when we want something. I like a good chat on the phone with my kids and I want to know about every part of their lives, the good as well as the bad, and I'm sure God does too.

The Tale

 I was struck by a song called 'The Tale' that our special guest, Diane Regan, sang on our last Gospel Tour. She can remember writing this song in Newcastledon, by the Scottish borders, in the summer of the year 2000. She had picked up a newspaper and jotted down some of the headlines and words that stood out. The first line, 'Excuse me, I've reason to believe that you've been sinking', was the story of a policeman on patrol near Ludgate Hill in London on a bike, who cycled through wet concrete and got stuck! Obviously the actual song is about something completely different, but since it was from a newspaper filled with stories (I think it was the *Daily Mail* of all papers), that's how the chorus and idea behind the wordplay on 'stories' and 'tale' came through.

Diane says that the whole song actually speaks for itself – that life does hurt, other people unfortunately do make judgements about what the best thing to do is, and they're sometimes not very tactful, but ultimately we do have a choice about the path we take and the best choice we could make is to take the journey with a good God who only wants the best for us!

THE TALE by Diane Regan

Excuse me, I've reason to believe, that you've been
    sinking!
Does it surprise you that it shows that much?
Well, don't throw the towel in, what a waste of time,
Don't you realize you need a happy ending!

Every story has to end some way,
Every lifetime has a story to say,
Everybody has a choice in the tale,
And not every tale has a sting.

You say that everywhere you turn
There's only heartache,
The look of love has not been seen for years.
And then you say we learn from our hurts,
Oh well, I think we've learnt enough for now!

Words

 Yes, it's a nice song, but it also makes the point that if I come over to you after a show and comment on what a wonderful family you have around you, a thrilling job, that

your kids are a credit to you, and that you have the best of friends, but then say how awful your hair looked, I could guarantee it would be the comment about your hair that you would remember when you went home that night! Apparently it takes 11 positive comments to overthrow the one negative remark that seems to stick in the mind for so long. It always makes me smile when I realize that it was God's positive words that created the world, and how sad it is when we use our tongues to be so critical. Let's be positive people today, creating not destroying.

A Critical Moment

Let's face the facts. No one is better than anyone else. So let's not pretend we have the right to criticize others. This makes a person think twice before judging someone:

Amateurs built the ark. Professionals built the *Titanic*. Stop passing judgement on one another (Romans 14, verse 13).

Apathy, Apathy, All Is Apathy

 If you do something enough times it becomes normality. My adultery became normality, my swearing became normality, my drinking became normality. Even if a husband and wife get into arguing too much, it can become normality after a while. Be careful. This is particularly true of 'spirituality apathy'. If we are apathetic Christians and not on fire for God, it will become normality. God did not give us a fresh life to do nothing with it. Every day with God should be new.

Just Passing By

 I like this anonymous poem, asking us to consider what it would be like if Jesus came to call on you today. Wow, what a thought!

Would you have to change your
   clothes before you let Him in?
Or hide some magazines, and put
   the Bible where they'd been?
Would you hide your worldly music
   and put some hymn books out?
Could you let Jesus walk right
   in, or would you rush about?
And I wonder – if the Saviour
   spent a day or two with you,
Would you go right on doing, the
   things you always do?
Would you go right on saying, the
   things you always say?
Or would life for you continue
   as it does from day to day?

Would you take Jesus with you
    everywhere you go?
Or would you maybe change your plans,
    Just for a day or so?
Would you be glad to have Him
    meet your closest friends?
Or would you hope they stay away,
    until his visit ends?
Would you be glad to have Him
    stay for ever on and on?
Or would you sigh with great
    relief when He at last was gone?
It might be interesting to know,
    the things that you would do,
If Jesus came in person, to spend
    some time with you.

MOT

 My wife Yvonne has become addicted to being tidy. Last night I got out to go to the loo at 2 a.m. and when I got back she'd made the bed! Seriously, though, it's very easy to get addicted to things. We can get addicted to television, sport, computers, cars, our businesses – almost anything. You can even get addicted to house-work, ladies. OK – well, not in your area then! But, joking apart, it's healthy to keep a regular look at our spiritual lives just like we do when we go to the GP to test our blood pressure or to the dentist for a check-up. When is your next spiritual MOT due?

Pack Up Your Troubles

Knowing God cares and that I can talk to him about anything has helped me through so many difficulties and problems, and I often wonder how others get through life without him. Not very long ago I was diagnosed with prostate cancer, and the support of my family and Christian friends around me was vital. I have seen God take people through their difficulties in miraculous ways. Believe me, handing over the struggles you face in life is the best way of dealing with them. I think this is why the Bible suggests that we have a simple faith, like that of a child. This reminds me of a wonderful story I was told about a little boy who is walking with his mother down the road when they pass a church.

'Who lives in that big house?' asks the boy.

'That's God's house,' replies the mother.

'Can I take a look inside?' asks the boy.

'Of course you can, the door's open,' she smiles.

The boy darts inside and about two minutes later he rushes out again.

'Did you see God?' enquires his mother.

The boy looks up and says, 'No, God's away. But his Mummy's scrubbing the floor.'

Ah So

Apparently an electric Japanese toilet seat newly available in the USA offers de-luxe comforts including heating, a water spray, fan and anti-bacterial glazing – all for only US$ 800! Why do we get so obsessed with luxury? I often come across people who wonder why life is so tough, almost as if they are the only ones being hard

done by. The fact is that we do live in a world that is dying and full of pain and anguish because humanity decided to carry on without the God who made each of us. The Bible has more to say about suffering than being triumphant, but shows that with God's help we can overcome and endure our difficulties. 'Even if I go through the deepest darkness, I will not be afraid, Lord, for you are with me. Your shepherd's rod and staff protect me.'

Over My Shoulder

My favourite bit in Psalm 23 says, 'Surely goodness and mercy shall follow me all the days of my life . . .' I like this King James version because it seems to suggest I should stop once in a while, look over my shoulder, and see how God's goodness and mercy have indeed been following me. Seeing what he has done in my past encourages me on into the future.

God's Bad Press

 Religion has done a lot of damage to Christianity. The difference is that religion is man-made, whereas Christianity is God-given. Religion is binding; Christianity is freedom. Religion is rules and regulations; Christianity is a one-to-one relationship. If you ever see a Christian with a face as long as a totem pole, tell them to buck up because they are doing God a disservice. Being a Christian is brilliant, exciting stuff. Let's live as though that is true and show how God is alive and bigger than all the old buildings that we sometimes try and imprison him in.

Proper Billing

Yes, I do agree with Bobby that some churches look very unwelcoming on the outside. In showbusiness we know that it's so important to have the billing looking and sounding right as otherwise no one will ever come in and see the show. I'm not for one moment suggesting we should turn our churches into theatres, or criticizing others, but when I look at some of the buildings that are supposed to represent God, I'm a bit ashamed. With peeling paint, notice boards falling apart with a strange old language on them, no wonder people think the Church has nothing to offer them today. I know that the 'Church' is not really a building, but instead the people in it, but do the passers-by understand that? Please can we think how we can use the creative skills of communication and technology that God has given us to turn the house of God from a dead building into something more resembling heaven?

Ministry of Funny Walks

My walk with God is not the same as yours. That's because we are all different and God treats us that way. He doesn't lump us all together like some crowd at a football match, but sees us as individuals.

All Year Round

My year-long prayer for you as an individual would be:

12 Months of Happiness
52 Weeks of Joy
365 Days of Success
8,760 Hours of Good Health
52,600 Minutes of Peace
31,536,000 Seconds of Love

Is God a Woman?

This is an enduring question. The Bible does show God's feminine side and God's wisdom in the Proverbs is personified as a female, but, for the most part, God has chosen to reveal himself in the Bible as having a male personage. However, in chapter 1 of Genesis we are told that man (meaning mankind – as opposed to 'a man') is created in the image of God, both male and female, 'So God created human beings, making them to be like himself. He created them male and female.'

Therefore, we should not be surprised if God has both a 'maleness' and 'femaleness' to him, so both men and women can relate to God. God could be considered as motherly (hen) and yet be called the Heavenly Father (which is what Scripture often calls him). God is both caring and nurturing, yet powerful and strong. Two parents in one!

Where God Wants You

 I'm grateful to Andy Wall who sent me a few accounts from real people who survived the attack on the Twin Towers in New York on 9/11. Note they are just little things:

A head of a company who was running late that day because his son started school.
Another fellow survived because it was his turn to bring the do-nuts.
Others survived because they were stuck in traffic.
Others survived because the public transport was running late, or their taxis didn't turn up.

The one that struck me was the man who put on a new pair of shoes that morning. He took the various means of transport to get to work, but before he got there he developed a blister on his foot. He stopped at a chemist's to buy a plaster which made him miss the lift.

So, next time when you are stuck in traffic, miss a train, a bus or even an escalator or you turn back to answer a ringing telephone – in fact, all the little things that can annoy you – think to yourself, perhaps this is exactly where God wants me to be at that moment! One of those little annoying things could save your life.

Important Things

 People will forget what you said. People will forget what you did . . . but people will never forget how you made them feel.

Laughter from Above

 I have a friend who was at church and during the hymn singing suddenly burst into laughter and couldn't stop. There was nothing he could think of that triggered this outburst, simply perhaps the presence of God. Can laughter be used in worship? I think so. The whole point of jokes about humanity is to recognize our imperfections; imperfections which remind us that we have to rely on God to get us through. We praise God for showing us our imperfections, and rejoice that despite these, he still loves us, although I am sure he also has a chuckle at us from time to time!

The Ostrich

 This silly story reminds me that we should always think before speaking!

A man walks into a restaurant with a full-grown ostrich behind him. As he sits, the waitress comes over and asks for their orders. The man says, 'I'll have a hamburger, fries and a coke', and turns to the ostrich and says, 'What's yours?' 'I'll have the same,' answers the ostrich. A short time later the waitress returns with the order. 'That will be £6.40 please,' she says and the man reaches into his pocket and pulls out the exact money for payment.

The next day, the man and the ostrich go again to the

restaurant and the man says, 'I'll have a hamburger, fries and a coke,' and the ostrich says, 'I'll have the same.' Once again, the man reaches into his pocket and pays with the exact money.

This becomes a routine until, late one evening, the two enter again. 'The usual?' asks the waitress. 'No, this is Friday night, so I will have a steak, baked potato and salad,' says the man. 'Same for me,' says the ostrich. A short time later the waitress comes with the order and says, 'That will be £12.62.' Once again the man pulls the exact change out of his pocket and places it on the table.

The waitress can't hold back her curiosity any longer. 'Excuse me, sir. How do you manage to come up with the exact change out of your pocket every time?' 'Well,' says the man, 'several years ago I was cleaning the attic and I found an old lamp. When I rubbed it, a genie appeared and offered me two wishes. My first wish was that if I ever had to pay for anything, I would just put my hand in my pocket and the right amount of money would always be there.' 'That's brilliant!' says the waitress. 'Most people would wish for a million dollars or something, but you'll always be as rich as you want for as long as you live!' 'That's right. Whether it's a gallon of milk or a Rolls-Royce, the exact money is always there,' says the man.

The waitress then asks, 'One other thing, sir, what's with the ostrich?' The man sighs, pauses, and answers, 'My second wish was for a tall chick with long legs, who agrees with everything I say.'

Mind Over Matter

 The way that God has made the human brain is quite astonishing. The weight of an average human brain is almost one bag of sugar and your skin weighs twice as much as your brain. Your brain consists of 60 per cent white matter and 40 per cent grey matter, and is approximately 75 per cent water. It consists of about 100 billion neurons! That's about 166 times the number of people on the planet, and it would take you approximately 3,171 years to count them all. The number of internal thought pathways that your brain is capable of producing is one followed by 10.5 million kilometres of standard typewritten zeros! The human brain is an amazing creation, and you can test it out here for yourself:

Aoccdrnig to rscheearch at Txes M&A Uinervtisy, it deosn't mttaer in waht oredr the ltteers in a wrod are, the olny iprmoetnt tihng is taht the frist and lsat ltteer be in the rghit pclae.

The rset can be a total mses and you can sitll raed it wouthit a porbelm. Tihs is bcuseae the huamn mnid deos not raed ervey lteter by istlef, but the wrod as a wlohe.

Man's Best Friend

This is a story with a pretty hard-hitting 'sting in the tail', so prepare yourself for the end.

A man and his dog were walking along a road. The man was enjoying the scenery, when it suddenly occurred to him that he was dead. He remembered dying, and that the dog walking beside him had been dead for years. He wondered where the road was leading them.

After a while, they came to a high, white stone wall along one side of the road. It looked like fine marble. At the top of a long hill, it was broken by a tall arch that glowed in the sunlight. When he was standing before it, he saw a magnificent gate in the arch that looked like mother of pearl, and the street that led to the gate looked like pure gold.

He and the dog walked towards the gate, and as he got closer, he saw a man at a desk to one side. When he was close enough, he called out, 'Excuse me, where are we?'

'This is heaven, sir,' the man answered.

'Wow! Would you happen to have some water?' the man asked.

'Of course, sir. Come right in, and I'll have some ice water brought right up.' The man gestured, and the gate began to open.

'Can my friend,' gesturing towards his dog, 'come in too?' the traveller asked.

'I'm sorry, sir, but we don't accept pets.'

The man thought for a moment and then turned back towards the road and continued the way he had been going with his dog.

After another long walk, and at the top of another long hill, he came to a dirt road that led through a farm gate that looked as if it had never been closed. There was no fence. As he approached the gate, he saw a man inside, leaning against a tree and reading a book.

'Excuse me!' he called to the reader. 'Do you have any water?'

'Yeah, sure, there's a pump over there.' The man pointed to a place that couldn't be seen from outside the gate. 'Come on in.'

'How about my friend here?' the traveller gestured to the dog.

'There should be a bowl by the pump.' They went through the gate and, sure enough, there was an old-fashioned hand pump with a bowl beside it. The traveller filled the bowl and took a long drink, then he gave some to the dog.

When they were full, he and the dog walked back towards the man who was standing by the tree waiting for them.

'What do you call this place?' the traveller asked.

'This is heaven,' was the answer.

'Well, that's confusing,' the traveller said. 'The man down the road said that was heaven too.'

'Oh, you mean the place with the gold street and pearly gates? Nope. That's Hell.'

'Doesn't it make you mad for them to use your name like that?'

'No. I can see how you might think so, but we're just happy that they screen out the ones who'll leave their best friends behind.'

More Than It Seems

 We do use the word 'love' very freely and it can mean many different things – I love your car; I love ice cream; I love you. It's all pretty confusing when we only have one word for it in English – *love*! The ancient Greeks were much more sensible and had several words to explain this most incredible of God's gifts. *Eros* is all about a physical, passionate and romantic love. *Philia* is a love associated with a strong friendship. *Storge* explains the sort of love we have for our children. *Agape* means a general love – such as a love of chocolate. This last kind

68

of love is the one that best describes the love that God has for us. This is because it is unconditional. We don't deserve it, we can't earn it, and we can't buy it. It's a free gift from heaven, whoever we are, wherever we are, whatever we are. The classic biblical text on this self-sacrificial love is the well-known biblical verse, John 3, verse 16:

> This is how we know what love is: Christ gave his life for us.

The Bible speaks of love as a set of attitudes and actions that are far broader than the concept of love as an emotion. Love is seen as a set of behaviours that humankind is encouraged to act out. We are urged not just to love our partners, or even our friends, but also to love our enemies. The Bible describes this type of active love in 1 Corinthians 13, verses 4–8:

> I may be able to speak the languages of human beings and even of angels, but if I have no love, my speech is no more than a noisy gong or a clanging bell. I may have the gift of inspired preaching; I may have all

knowledge and understand all secrets; I may have all the faith needed to move mountains – but if I have no love, I am nothing. I may give away everything I have, and even give up my body to be burned – but if I have no love, this does me no good. Love is patient and kind; it is not jealous or conceited or proud; love is not ill mannered or selfish or irritable; love does not keep a record of wrongs; love is not happy with evil, but is happy with the truth. Love never gives up; and its faith, hope and patience never fail. Love is eternal.

This is the verse that is so often read out at weddings but, as we can see, it's meant to be used much wider than just with our spouses. Let's put the deeper love into action today.

Easy Peasy

 Girls, did you know that if you go clothes shopping and try things on, it burns up around 100 calories an hour? What a wonderful way to exercise! It shows that keeping fit doesn't always need to be a chore, but I understand how some feel that praying or reading their Bibles can be seen as a bit of a drag too, but it doesn't need to be like that. A friend of mine sets his alarm clock 20 minutes earlier than he needs it each morning, so that he can spend that time lying all snuggled up and warm talking to God. What a nice way to start the day.

Heavenly Texts

 I like this New Year text message sent to me, which I think is relevant all-year round:

4give quickly, love truly, laugh uncontrollably & expect a new year bursting with potential & wonderful heavenly surprises just for you. x

It's good to inspire one another.

Heavenly Mathematics

 The best mathematical equation I have ever seen sums up the whole gospel in one line:

$1 \times$ cross $+ 3 \times$ nails $= 4$ given

Talk Proper

 An article in an Australian magazine calculated that sending the entire Bible by text would take more than 30,000 messages and cost almost £3,440 at 10p for each message. You could buy around 1,500 pints of beer for that, which is what I suspect most people would prefer. However, it's amazing how the Bible is relevant today in every form and the Bible Society in Australia claims to be the first to translate all 31,173 verses of the Bible into text. Here's an example of the Bible in today's latest language: 'U, Lord, r my shepherd. I will neva be in need. U let me rest in fields of green grass. U lead me 2 streams of peaceful water' (Psalm 23, verses 1–2).

Here's my own message to you: 'Cannon & baL knO dat God Luvs dem & he Luvs U jst az much.'

An Interview With God

 I am so used to being interviewed now that it's usually an easy thing to do, but I was wondering what I would say if I ever got the chance to interview God. Then a friend sent me this poem, and it's blown my mind and many of my preconceptions right out of the water:

I dreamed I had an interview with God.
'So you would like to interview me?' God asked.
'If you have the time,' I said.
God smiled. 'My time is eternity. What questions do you have in mind for me?'
'What surprises you most about humankind?'
God answered . . .

'That they get bored with childhood,
they rush to grow up, and then
long to be children again.
'That they lose their health to make money . . .
and then lose their money to restore their health.

'That by thinking anxiously about the future,
they forget the present,
such that they live in neither
the present nor the future.

'That they live as if they will never die,
and die as though they had never lived.'

God's hand took mine
and we were silent for a while.

And then I asked . . .
'As a parent, what are some of life's lessons
you want your children to learn?'

'To learn they cannot make anyone
love them. All they can do
is let themselves be loved.

'To learn that it is not good
to compare themselves to others.

'To learn to forgive
by practising forgiveness.

'To learn that it only takes a few seconds
to open profound wounds in those they love,
and it can take many years to heal them.

'To learn that a rich person
is not one who has the most,
but is one who needs the least.

'To learn that there are people
who love them dearly,
but simply have not yet learned
how to express or show their feelings.

'To learn that two people can
look at the same thing
and see it differently.

'To learn that it is not enough that they
forgive one another, but they must also forgive
    themselves.'

'Thank you for your time,' I said humbly. 'Is there
anything else you would like your children to know?'

God smiled and said, 'Just know that I am here . . .
always.'

Just As I Am

Although I'm not a great lover of man-made religion, I think there is so much to learn from the Church of the past. This wonderful old hymn written by Charlotte Elliott in 1839 reminds me in such a graphic and moving way that I can come to God quite simply as I am. What a relief!

Just as I am without one plea
But that Thy blood was shed for me
And that Thou biddst me come to Thee
O Lamb of God, I come, I come!

Just as I am and waiting not
To rid my soul of one dark blot;
To Thee, whose blood can cleanse each spot,
O Lamb of God, I come, I come!

Just as I am, Thou wilt receive,
Wilt welcome, pardon, cleanse, relieve;
Because Thy promise I believe,
O Lamb of God, I come, I come!

Just as I am, Thy love unknown
Hath broken every barrier down;
Now, to be Thine, yes, Thine alone,
Oh Lamb of God, I come, I come!

Xmas

I used to hate using the word 'Xmas' instead of 'Christmas', trying to resist taking the 'Christ' out of 'Christmas' any more than it is already. However, I discovered that the early Christians used to use a secret 'fish' sign to each other as the Greek word for 'fish' (IXOYE) is also an acronym. I = JESUS, X = CHRIST, O = GOD, Y = SON, E = SAVIOUR. That X, then, means Christ, and so it really does mean something in the word 'Xmas'. Perhaps we can find a way of letting more people know.

Mother's Christmas Gifts

This funny story reminds me of how easy it is to get hold of the 'wrong end of the stick':

Four brothers left home for college, and they became successful doctors and lawyers and prospered. Some years later, they chatted after having dinner together. They discussed the gifts that they were able to give to their elderly mother who lived far away in another city.

The first, Milton, said, 'I had a big house built for Mother.'

The second, Michael, said, 'I had a £100,000 theatre built in the house.'

The third, Marvin, said, 'I had my Mercedes dealer deliver her an SL600.'

The fourth, Melvin, said, 'Listen to this. You know how Mum loved reading the Bible, and you know she can't read it any more because she can't see very well. I met this priest who told me about a parrot that can recite the entire Bible. It took 20 priests 12 years to teach him. I had to pledge to contribute £100,000 a year for 20 years to the church, but it was worth it. Mum just has to name the chapter and verse and the parrot will recite it.'

The other brothers were impressed.

After the holidays, Mum sent out her 'thank you' notes.

She wrote: 'Milton, the house you built is so huge. I live in only one room, but I have to clean the whole house. Thanks anyway.'

'Michael, you give me an expensive theatre with Dolby sound, it could hold 50 people, but all my friends are dead, I've lost my hearing, and I'm nearly blind. I'll never use it. Thank you for the gesture just the same.'

'Marvin, I am too old to travel. I stay at home; I have my groceries delivered, so I never use the Mercedes. The thought was good. Thanks.'

'Dearest Melvin, you were the only son to have the good sense to give a little thought to your gift. The chicken was delicious. Thank you.'

The Night Before Jesus Came

This is a wonderfully clever re-write by an unknown author of the classic poem about Father Christmas, but as the season has more to do with the birth of Jesus Christ than a man in a red suit, I think I prefer this:

T'was the night before Jesus and all through the
    house,
Not a creature was praying, not one in the house.
Their Bibles were lain on the shelf without care,
In hopes that Jesus would not stop by there.

The children were dressing to crawl into bed,
Not one ever kneeling, or bowing a head.
And Mum in her rocker with a babe on her lap,
Was watching the *Late Show* while I took a nap.

When out of the East there arose such a clatter,
I sprang to my feet to see what was the matter.
Away to the window I flew like a flash,
Tore open the shutters and threw up the sash!

When what to my wondering eyes should appear,
But angels proclaiming that Jesus was here.
With a light like the sun sending forth a bright ray,
I knew in a moment this must be THE DAY!

The light of His face made me cover my head.
It was Jesus! Returning just like He said.
And though I possessed worldly wisdom and wealth,
I cried when I saw Him in spite of myself.

In the Book of Life, which He held in His hand,
Was written the name of every saved man.

He spoke not a word as He searched for my name;
When He said, 'It's not here' . . . my head hung in
  shame.

The people whose names had been written with love,
He gathered to take to His Father above.
With those who were ready, He rose without sound,
While all the rest were left standing around.

I fell to my knees, but it was too late;
I had waited too long and thus sealed my fate.
I stood and I cried as they rose out of sight;
Oh, if only we had been prepared for this night.

In the words of this poem the meaning is clear;
The time for His coming is drawing near.
There's only one life and when comes the last call.
We'll find what He told us was true after all.

The Three Wise Women

You do know what would have happened if it had been three wise women instead of men, don't you?

They would have asked for directions,
arrived on time,
helped deliver the baby,
cleaned the stable,
made a casserole,
and brought disposable nappies as gifts!

Too Busy to Pray

Someone once said, 'If you are too busy to pray, you are too busy!' It's probably true because we can pray anywhere at any time. We don't need a phone line, broadband or a satellite dish, because we have an immediate and free connection. I know life can be incredibly busy with so many demands, so I try and chat to God on a regular basis throughout my day. My favourite two-minute prayer is when I sit quietly for a few moments, letting go of all the burdens and anxieties that are so much a part of life. Then I let my heart speak to God. You don't need special words or prayers. Just tell God what you are feeling. It's often the most refreshing two minutes of my day.

Did You Listen?

I wrote this to remind myself that we are sometimes so bad at hearing God:

He said 'I am here'
Did you listen or just say 'where'?
He said 'I died for you'
Did you listen, or didn't you really care?
He said 'the nails hurt me as they were driven
  through my hand'
Did you listen and have compassion? Or didn't you
  understand?
He said 'I am the son of God and I came to love you'
Did you listen or say 'not yet, I have many things to
  do'?
He said 'come to me and let all your troubles be
  mine'
Did you listen or say 'no thanks, it's OK, I'm doing
  all right, in fact I'm fine'?
He said 'let me help you because I am the great I am'
Did you listen or say 'no thanks, I don't need anyone,
  because I am my own man'?
When the end days come and it's the end of time for
  men
I just wonder silently to myself, will you listen then?

Under No Illusion

Someone once said that God is never disillusioned with us as he has no illusions about us in the first place!

A Proper Drink

 I'm told there is a strange plant in South Africa which finds a moist place and send its roots down and becomes green for a while until the place becomes dry, when it draws itself out and rolls itself up and is blown along by the wind until it comes to another moist place, where it repeats the same process. On and on the plant goes, stopping wherever it finds a little water until the spot is dry. In the end, after all its wanderings, it is nothing but a bundle of dry roots and leaves. It's a sad story, but I know some people like that. Continually searching for something to make them satisfied, but nothing seems to work. I call them the 'if only's'. 'If only I could win something on the Lottery everything would be fine'; 'If only I could meet the right person, I would be happy'; 'If only I could get that promotion, I wouldn't ask for anything else.' The thing is, we all know it isn't true. Satisfaction never seems to come from money and possessions and I know plenty of rich and famous people who are still searching for happiness just like that African plant. In my experience there is only one thing that will quench a deep longing which comes from within, and that's the spiritual satisfaction that only God can give. Make sure we all take a big gulp of it today, and every day.

Jesus answered, 'Those who drink this water will get thirsty again, but those who drink the water that I will give them will never be thirsty again. The water that I will give them will become in them a spring which will provide them with life-giving water and give them eternal life' (John 4, verse 14).

Grumble Not

If, like me, you find it far too easy to start grumbling, I dedicate this funny poem to you:

There's a family nobody likes to meet;
They live, it is said, on Complaining Street
In the city of Never-Are-Satisfied,
The River of Discontent beside.

They growl at that and they growl at this;
Whatever comes, there is something amiss;
And whether their station be high or humble,
They are all known by the name of Grumble.

The weather is always too hot or cold;
Summer and winter alike they scold.
Nothing goes right with the folks you meet
Down on that gloomy Complaining Street.

They growl at the rain and they growl at the sun;
In fact, their growling is never done.
And if everything pleased them, there isn't a doubt
They'd growl that they'd nothing to grumble about!

But the queerest thing is that not one of the same
Can be brought to acknowledge his family name;
For never a Grumbler will own that he
Is connected with it at all, you see.

The worst thing is that if anyone stays
Among them too long, he will learn their ways;
And before he dreams of the terrible jumble
He's adopted into the family of Grumble.

And so it were wisest to keep our feet
From wandering into Complaining Street;
And never to growl, whatever we do,
Lest we be mistaken for Grumblers, too.

Let us learn to walk with a smile and a song,
No matter if things do sometimes go wrong;
And then, be our station high or humble,
We'll never belong to the family of Grumble!

Wise Words

I love that Bible verse that asks God to put a guard on my mouth. Sometimes I am too quick to answer a friend in need and try to come up with a quick-fix solution, when in fact I could be listening and empathizing with how he really feels as this anonymous internet blog reveals:

After I started listening to the people I talk to . . .
and listen to what they had to say . . .
instead of just waiting for my turn to talk . . .
and listening . . .
like really really listening, it's the best thing you can
    do for a friend . . .
just being there . . .
and soaking in everything they say . . .
it's nice . . .
'cause then people know they can talk to you . . .
and they will be more likely to talk to you . . .
and tell you things . . .
so you get to know them better . . .
and that's just really nice . . .

God Is Still Working on Me

 I suppose we must be careful of not taking ourselves too seriously. Church people are sometimes too pious, and that is when I think God uses humour to remind us that we are not as important and as perfect as maybe we think we are. Here are a few of my favourite church gaffs:

Our enthusiastic curate was leading a service and read some banns of marriage. He was always one to encourage taking part, and said, 'If anyone knows of any reason in law why these people should not be married, that would be great.'

An irregularity at the enthronement of Roy Williamson as Bishop of Southwark was very funny when, throughout the long and complex service, Bishop Roy had been ably chaplained by the young succentor, Fr Nigel Worn, juggling books, crozier, mitre, etc., and generally steering his new bishop around the cathedral. At the end of the service, Bishop Roy stepped forward for a few informal words of thanks to all the people who had contributed to the day. '. . . and a special word of thanks to Father Nigel, who had his hand up my back, twiddling my knobs . . .'

Let Me Help You

I do think God has a sense of humour. After all, he made us! There are lots of funny incidents in the Bible, but preserving humour through translations from Aramaic to Greek to Latin to English is problematic, but with a little sympathy for the intentions of the speaker, you can find a lot, and I'm sure Jesus used humour in his sermons. What can be a funnier example than when Jesus talks about the man trying to take a speck out of his brother's eye when he has a plank in his own?

Funny When You Know

I'm told that the passage with the most gags in the Bible is from John 1, verses, 45–51, and I'm quite excited to know that a Bible scholar took the trouble to point out where the gags or jokes would have been. Even though it's pretty difficult for us to understand why it's funny because of the difference in culture and the changes that history has made, I'm so pleased to know that there is plenty of hidden humour in the Bible if you take the trouble to look. This is the piece in John:

Philip found Nathaniel and told him, 'We have found the one whom Moses wrote about in the book of the Law and whom the prophets also wrote about. He is Jesus son of Joseph, from Nazareth.' 'Can anything good come from Nazareth?' Nathaniel asked. (Joke.). 'Come and see,' answered Philip. When Jesus saw Nathaniel coming to him, he said about him, 'Here is a real Israelite; there is nothing false in him!' ('Hey, here's an honest Jew' – joke.) Nathaniel (not getting it) asked him, 'How do you know me?' Jesus answered, 'I saw you when you were under the fig tree before Philip called you.' (Big joke.) 'Teacher,' answered Nathaniel, 'you are the Son of God! You are the King of Israel!' Jesus said, 'Do you believe just because I told you I saw you when you were under the fig tree? You will see much greater things than this!' And he said to them, 'I am telling you the truth: you will see heaven open and God's angels going up and coming down on the Son of Man.'

Printer's Error

The odd Bible word has been liable to human error down the ages. A Bible printed in Cambridge in 1805 had the proof-reader query a comma and the editor pencilled in 'to remain'; as a result, Galatians 4, verse 29 read, 'he that was born after the flesh persecuted him that was born after the spirit to remain, even so it is now'.

?/.

Don't put a question mark where God puts a full stop.

The Mouths of Babes

This is the true result, with no alterations, of a recent school exam paper on the subject of the Bible.

It's quite hilarious:

In the first book of the Bible, Guinessis, God got tired of creating the world, so He took the Sabbath off. Adam and Eve were created from an apple tree.

Noah's wife was called Joan of Ark. Noah built an ark, which the animals came on to in pears.

Lot's wife was a pillar of salt by day, but a ball of fire by night.

The Jews were a proud people and throughout history they had trouble with the unsympathetic Genitals.

Samson was a strongman who let himself be led astray by a Jezebel like Delilah. Samson slayed the Philistines with the axe of the apostles.

Moses led the Hebrews to the Red Sea, where they made unleavened bread, which is bread made without any ingredients. The Egyptians were all drowned in the dessert. Afterwards, Moses went up on Mount Cyanide to get the Ten Amendments. The First Commandment was when Eve told Adam to eat the apple. The Fifth Commandment is to humour thy father and mother. The seventh Commandment is thou shalt not admit adultery.

Moses died before he ever reached Canada. Then Joshua led the Hebrews in the battle of Geritol.

The greatest miracle in the Bible is when Joshua told his son to stand still and he obeyed him.

David was a Hebrew king skilled at playing the liar. He fought with the Finklesteins, a race of people who lived in Biblical times. Solomon, one of

David's sons, had 300 wives and 700 porcupines.

Jesus enunciated the Golden Rule, which says to do one to others before they do one to you. He also explained, 'Man doth not live by sweat alone.'

The people who followed the Lord were called the 12 decibels. The epistles were the wives of the apostles. One of the opossums was St Matthew who was, by profession, a taximan.

St Paul cavorted to Christianity. He preached holy acrimony, which is another name for marriage. A Christian should have only one wife. This is called monotony.

Bearing All

A child came home from Sunday school and told his mother that he had learned a new song about a cross-eyed bear named Gladly. It took his mother a while before she realized that the hymn was really 'Gladly The Cross I'd Bear'.

Dear God

I love the simplicity of a child's faith. No wonder the Bible says we should have a faith like theirs. Here's a selection of my favourite letters to God:

Dear God
Instead of letting people die and having to make new ones, why don't you just keep the ones you already have?
Cindy

Dear God
Who draws the lines around countries?
Nan

Dear God
What does it mean you are a Jealous God? I thought you had everything.
Robert

Dear God
Why is Sunday school on Sunday? I thought it was supposed to be our day of rest.
Tom

Dear God
I went to this wedding and they kissed in church. Is that OK?
Neil

Dear God
The bad people laughed at Noah – 'You made an ark on dry land, you fool'.
But he was smart, he stuck with You. That's what I would do.
Edward

Winner

 The most Oscars ever won by anyone was Walt Disney who got 26. An amazing feat, but not as incredible as the thought that God loves you even more than an Oscar. Why else would he count the hairs on your head! The Bible says he even counts the hairs on our heads. At least it doesn't take him too long to count Tommy's then!

Favourites

Funnily enough, my favourite comedians have always been double acts. Laurel & Hardy, Abbot and Costello, Dean Martin & Jerry Lewis had me in stitches. Laughter makes you feel high, and when I get on stage and start to hear people laugh, I automatically start laughing along with them. It soon becomes a party without the need for alcohol or drugs. In fact, laughter is like a drug because it brings about such a change. It's one drug that we recommend everyone should take on a regular basis!

For Ever

Tommy Cooper, Max Wall and Fred Emny used to make me laugh, but these days I really like Lee Evans and Peter Kay. It's so important that comedy is passed down from one generation to the next. God put laughter in our DNA. There's always been laughter and it will be there for ever, particularly when we get to heaven when it says that there will be no more tears and we shall be full of joy. I can't wait!

Best Medicine

I believe that laughter is God's medicine for a hurting world. The medicine works even if you are feeling really ill. There's been several times when I have had a terrible bout of flu or bronchitis and felt absolutely awful. As soon as I went on stage, the illness just dropped off me and I felt fine. As soon as I came off, it all flooded back. No wonder they call performing laughter 'Dr Adrenaline'. When you laugh, you forget all your problems. Laughter brings a sort of inner peace, and because of that we believe that there is no doubt that laughter comes from God. All the joyous things in life are from him, which is why music and laughter go so well together. I'm sure God laughs at our act too! Particularly when it goes wrong!

LOL

Here are a few of the best quotes explaining why hilarity is so good for you. When you read these you will understand why it's so important to keep laughing:

Laughter increases production of immunoglobulins, antibodies which boost the immune system.
(Robert Holden-founder of first NHS Laughter Clinic)

100 laughs a day gives you as much beneficial exercise as 10 minutes of rowing.
(Dr William Fry, Stanford Medical School)

Regular laughter permanently lowers your heart rate and blood pressure.
(Dr Annette Goodheart, Independent Laughter Therapist)

Being cheerful keeps you healthy. It is slow death to be gloomy all the time.

(The Bible)

He will fill your mouth with laughter.

(The Bible)

On Tap

 A cat and a mouse died on the same day and went up to heaven. At the top they met God and he asked them, 'How do you like it so far?'

The mouse replied, 'It's great, but can I get a pair of roller skates?' God said 'Sure', and he gave him a pair of roller skates.

The next day God saw the cat and asked him, 'How do you like it up here so far?' and the cat replied, 'Great, I didn't know you had meals-on-wheels up here!'

The Best Policy

 I used to worry about verse 16 in James 5, which says, 'So then, confess your sins to one another and pray for one another, so that you will be healed.' It all seemed a bit heavy to me, and I certainly didn't want to expose myself to people I didn't know very well. Then I discovered that actually this verse is more about honesty. Honesty is important. Honesty is having a clear conscience with myself and with my fellow human beings. Honesty is about being open with God, who knows just what I am like anyway, and knowing that he still loves me. Someone said, 'Always tell the truth. Even if you have to make it up.' It makes life a whole lot easier to be honest and, as Mark Twain said, 'If you tell the truth you don't have to remember anything.'

Porkie-Pies

 Comic writer Tad Williams says, 'We tell lies when we are afraid . . . afraid of what we don't know, afraid of what others will think, afraid of what will be found out about us. But every time we tell a lie, the thing that we fear grows stronger.' I think I would agree with that.

Don't Give Up

 I can't count the times I've been at my wits' end and ready to turn around and forget it all. Most of the time I'm glad I didn't, as giving in on the spur of the moment when I'm feeling low isn't the best time to think things through properly and make the best decision – as this poem shows:

When things go wrong, as they sometimes will,
When the road you're trudging seems all uphill,
When the funds are low and the debts are high,
And you want to smile, but you have to sigh,
When care is pressing you down a bit
Rest if you must, but don't you quit.

Life is queer with its twists and its turns,
As every one of us sometimes learns,
And many a failure turns about

When they might have won, had they stuck it out.
Don't give up though the pace seems slow,
You may succeed with another blow.

Often the struggler has given up
When he might have captured the victors cup;
And he learned too late when the night came down,
How close he was to the golden crown.

Success is failure turned inside out
The silver tint of the clouds of doubt
And you never can tell how close you are,
It may be near when it seems so far;
So stick to the fight when you're hardest hit,
It's when things seem worst that you mustn't quit!

God of History

 Physicists now believe the universe to be three billion years younger than previously thought. New information gathered by the Hipparcos satellite, combined with a re-analysis of other distance data, has enabled researchers to refine the lower age limit of the universe to 9.6 billion years. Wow! I never knew that God was that old!

Creative Power

 Some 71 per cent of the Earth's surface is covered with water. The Earth is estimated to weigh 6,585,600,000,000,000,000,000 tons, while the area of the Earth is almost 200 million square miles, and travels through space at 66,700 miles per hour. Earth is the only planet in the

Solar System known to be geologically active, with earthquakes and volcanoes forming the landscape, replenishing carbon dioxide into the atmosphere and erasing impact craters from meteors. The Solar System is a name we give to a star and its family of planets, moons, asteroids, meteors and comets. At the moment, there are 12 known Solar Systems in our galaxy, the Milky Way. This means that there are 12 stars in the Milky Way known to have planets spinning around them. It's a big world, a vast universe, and a colossal God. No wonder Psalms 8, verses 3–4, talks about God placing the stars in space: 'When I look at the sky, which you have made, at the moon and the stars, which you set in their places, what are human beings, that you think of them; mere mortals, that you care for them?' God must have really big hands. These same hands are the ones that keep me safe and secure every day.

God's Name

A little boy was asked by his teacher what he thought God's name was.

'Oh, that's easy,' the boy replied, 'His name is Andy.'

'What makes you think his name is Andy?' the teacher asked incredulously.

'Well, you see at church we used to sing this song "Andy walks with me, Andy talks with me".'

Thirteen

Triskaidekaphobia, fear of the number 13, dates back to Nordic mythology. But the combination of Friday and the number 13 seems to have originated with Christ, whose last supper before his arrest supposedly seated 13 and he was crucified on a Friday.

Superstition

I don't believe in superstition. It brings bad luck. Actually it's quite interesting to see where some of these old worries come from. In the theatre we have an old tradition never to whistle on stage. This is simply because sailors were often used as part-time fly-men and would communicate with each other with a whistle. If you whistled on stage you were likely to find a backcloth containing a huge iron bar dropped on your head. Churchgoers are sometimes the source of superstitions too. For example, crossing your fingers is making the sign of the Christian faith with your fingers so that evil spirits would be prevented from destroying our chances of good fortune.

We say 'God Bless You' when somebody sneezes. When the great plague swept Europe, sufferers began sneezing violently, which was a sign of death. The Pope therefore passed a law requiring people to bless the sneezer. At the same time, it was expected that anybody sneezing would cover his or her mouth with a cloth or their hand. This was obviously to stop the spreading of the disease, but many believed that it was to keep the soul intact. Sneezing 'into the air' would allow the soul to escape, and death would be imminent. Up until this time, the opposite was true. Those who sneezed were congratulated, as it was believed that a violent sneeze would expel evil from their bodies. Armed with this sort of understanding, we can happily put a lot of these dead myths behind us, and carry on with the reality of enjoying a relationship with a living God.

Holy Who?

 The whole idea of a God made up of three people can be difficult to contemplate, but someone once described it to me as understanding how water can be in the form of ice, steam or liquid. They are all water, but in different forms, and each with different roles. So it is with God the Father, God the Son, and God the Holy Spirit.

Keeping It Simple

 We do seem to have a tendency to make explaining our faith very complicated. I know a man who's spent his whole life carrying a cross everywhere he goes. He's not an idiot, or deranged, but is eager to let as many people as possible see a visual symbol of what God has done for us. Arthur Blessitt recently completed a historic and unprecedented crosswalk in every nation on Earth. He has carried on foot a 12 foot cross for Jesus around the world since 1969 – through wars, deserts, jungles, 307 countries, seven continents and 37,352 miles (60,099 kilometres). The *Guinness Book of World Records 1996–2007* lists this as 'The World's Longest Walk'. This modern-day pilgrim has faced a firing squad, been arrested 24 times, been through 50 countries at war, fasted 40 days, ran for President of the USA, and has walked with 70,000 people across Poland. He has been on all major news programmes worldwide. Billy Graham has walked with him, Pope John Paul II has welcomed him to Rome, Yasser Arafat welcomed him to Beirut, and he has slept in Prime Minister Begin's house in Israel. He carried the cross through such places as Iraq, North Korea, Iran, Afghanistan, Somalia, Sudan, Russia, China, South Africa, Lebanon, India, Antarctica, Palestine, Israel, Cuba, Libya, Yemen, Vietnam and Mongolia, etc. He has now been on the longest journey in the history of the world. Having done all this, Arthur, who was born in 1943, says, 'I love God and I love people. I try to keep it simple.'

Just Great

'God doesn't want us to do great things, only small things with great love.'
(Anon.)

Who Loves Ya, Baby?

The next time you feel as if God can't use you, remember the following people:

NOAH was a drunk . . .
ABRAHAM was too old . . .

98

ISAAC was a daydreamer . . .
JACOB was a liar . . .
LEAH was ugly . . .
JOSEPH was abused.
MOSES couldn't talk . . .
GIDEON was afraid . . .
SAMSON had long hair, and was a womanizer!
RAHAB was a prostitute . . .
JEREMIAH and TIMOTHY were too young . . .
DAVID had an affair and was a murderer . . .
ELIJAH was suicidal . . .
ISAIAH preached naked . . .
JONAH ran from God . . .
NAOMI was a widow . . .
JOB went bankrupt . . .
JOHN the Baptist ate bugs . . .
PETER denied Christ . . .
The DISCIPLES fell asleep while praying . . .
MARTHA worried about everything . . .
MARY MAGDALENE was demon possessed . . .
The SAMARITAN WOMAN was divorced . . . more
than once!!
ZACCHEUS was too small . . .
PAUL was too religious . . .
TIMOTHY had an ulcer . . .
and
LAZARUS WAS DEAD!!!!

I Don't Believe It!

 It's odd how some of us spend our whole lives searching for God, and then expend the rest of our lives trying to convince ourselves that God really does love us. I think this is because our emotions often get in the way. Perhaps we need to realize that our emotions don't always tell us the truth. As the wonderful evangelist Billy Graham once said:

> Our emotions are God-given, and life would be very dull without them, but sometimes they get confused and make us believe things that aren't really true. There may be all sorts of reasons for this, including the way we were raised or our childhood experiences – but whatever the reason, our emotions aren't always dependable guides. The only solution is to let the truth be your guide, even if your emotions tell you otherwise. And what is the truth? The truth is God loves you. Yes, He is holy and pure, but despite our sins, He still loves us. Just as parents still love their children even if they disobey, so God loves us even if we sin.

Battle Plan

 It's easy to imagine Satan as some sort of pantomime baddie who doesn't really have any power and just hangs around snarling at us. It's just as easy to treat him as if he has all the power and we end up living in fear of what he might do in our lives. I think the truth is somewhere between the two. We must remember that Satan hates God and hates us too because we are made in God's image. Nevertheless, he is only a fallen angel and his limited authority and power is under the direct control of God himself.

You and Whose Army?

Sometimes we blame the enemy for everything that goes wrong which I think gives him far too much credit! If we blame him too much, this may also mean that we are avoiding taking some responsibility ourselves. We are just as able to make a mess of things without Satan's help! So let's keep the battle in perspective, remembering most importantly of all that our struggle may be against the 'principalities and powers', but it says in 2 Chronicles 20, verse 15 that the battle is God's. 'Jahaziel said, "Your Majesty and all you people of Judah and Jerusalem, the LORD says that you must not be discouraged or be afraid to face this large army. The battle depends on God, not on you."' That's Good News then.

A Sermon About Lying

A minister told his congregation, 'Next week I plan to preach about the sin of lying. To help you understand my sermon, I want you all to read Mark 17.'

The following Sunday, as he prepared to deliver his sermon, the minister asked for a show of hands. He wanted to know how many had read Mark 17. Every hand went up. The minister smiled and said, 'Mark has only 16 chapters. I will now proceed with my sermon on the sin of lying.'

God's Army

A friend was in front of me coming out of church one day, and the Pastor was standing at the door as usual to shake hands. He grabbed my friend by the hand and pulled him aside. The Pastor said to him, 'You need to join the Army of the Lord!'

My friend replied, 'I'm already in the Army of the Lord, Pastor.'

So the Pastor questioned, 'Then how come I don't see you except at Christmas and Easter?'

He whispered back, 'I'm in the Secret Service.'

Not Guilty!

If there is one thing that the Devil will do everything in his power to make us feel, it's guilt. I used to feel really guilty about a lot of things, and no matter how much I drank it never got rid of it. I found the only way was to let God take away my guilt and set me free from it. Sometimes, though, even after giving it to God, we still feel guilty, but we don't need to. It's worth remembering that there are two types of guilt: false guilt, which comes from other people's judgements, and true guilt, which comes from divine judgement. The Devil uses false guilt to keep us from God, because we feel too bad to approach him. God uses true guilt to stir up our consciences and remind us to act responsibly, so it's not meant to make us feel condemned, but to act as a positive motivator. It does not mean that we will never get it wrong, or make mistakes, but all we have to do is tell God how we feel, accept his forgiveness again, and move on. There is not a single verse in the Bible that says we should feel depressed, rejected or worthless. We are truly forgiven, so what could be better? In the Bible there is a verse, Romans 8, verse 1, which says, 'There is therefore now no condemnation to them which are in Christ Jesus . . .'

One-Way

Never give the Devil a ride – he will always want to drive.

Jungle Matters

Did you see me in the jungle? Making that *I'm A Celebrity Get Me Out Of Here!* was quite fun, but it was pretty rough. Some people seemed to think that the cameras got turned off and we all disappeared into a luxury hotel, but we didn't. What you saw on television was what actually happens. I got bitten everywhere. I had spider bites and mosquito bites. I was starving hungry, but

had constipation and the trots at the same time! I didn't know whether I was coming or going. Everybody in the camp reacted differently. Some took to it like a kangaroo's pouch; others hated it and couldn't wait to be voted out. It reminded me that we are all different. God is an amazing craftsman, who doesn't take short cuts. He is a God of variety. He didn't make all the plants the same colour, shape or size, and neither did he us. Each one of us is unique. Let's remember to celebrate the difference.

Spiritual Amnesia

 Spiritual amnesia can be very common among Christians. Most of the time it's very unintentional on our part, but none the less it happens. The Devil makes us forget what manner of person we were before Christ saved us. He gives us little 'comfort zones' to be content in, so we don't feel the need for God. Then as we lounge around in an idle state, the Devil steals our purpose that God has given us. We need to have a repentive heart and come back to the Lord, and God will be 'just to forgive us' and restore to us his purpose in our lives. This poem by Timothy Jon Barrett reminds us of who we really are.

Have you ever lost your thoughts,
just forgotten who you are?
A total lapse of memory,
your brain not up to par.

These strange and scary feelings,
that frequently will seize ya,
the inner person drifts away,
from a spiritual amnesia.

Those attacks come straight from Satan,
he makes you to forget,
a partial lapse at first,
then he steals it – bit by bit.

'Cause a Christian needs his memory,
to remember who he is,
those thoughts that keep you going,
Satan wants them to be his.

The item that he wants the most,
is remembrance of salvation,
'Just rest a while,' he tells you,
'give your soul a good vacation.'

Then once you've packed your bags,
and journeyed on this trip,
then Satan steals your purpose,
and tightens down his grip.

Then the farther on you go,
the distance you have travelled,
vacation time starts piling up,
and your memory's been unravelled.

Then in the midst of leisure,
the fun you've had so far,
you can't recall for the life of you,
your home, or who you are.

But the thought it lingers firmly,
that you've jumped the chosen track,
how did I get to where I am?
– and how do I get back?

First cancel your vacation,
pack your bags, start getting ready,
concentrate on Jesus Christ,
bring those thoughts back firm and steady.

Then keep your thoughts on Jesus,
wherever you may roam,
and don't forget your purpose,
if you travel far from home.

'Cause Jesus loves the forgetful,
when repentance they do find,
so remember who you are, my friend,
and keep Jesus on your mind.

Sussed

Atheism is a non-prophet organization.

Rock Around the Church

There's nothing I like better than taking our Gospel Show out on the road. It takes many different forms, but most recently has been called 'Rock Around the Church'. The show is produced as a fully professional evening with lighting effects, sound crew, a band and our special guest stars. It's a way of combining great music and comedy with a cringe-free look at life and faith. We've been doing the show for several years now and every time we see people get touched in so many different ways, whether it's seeing their faith revived, gaining a greater understanding of how much God loves them, or meeting God in a personal way for the first time. I must say that there's no greater encouragement than to see God at work in someone's life.

They're Behind You

I love the title of our Gospel Show, 'Rock Around the Church' because it offers the double image of the Church being built on a Rock that is solid and dependable, and rock 'n' roll music, which we love to perform to show how Christians can have a really good time. We do the show in large churches or theatres, and I remember one old church near Birmingham which we lovingly and respectfully transformed with our lighting and sound systems for the evening to make it an attractive and comfortable place for those who wouldn't normally come into a church. The only problem with the old church was that we had to use the outside graveyard area as a dressing room because there was not enough

room for us all in the vestry at the back. We spent the whole evening doing silly graveyard gags on and off stage and had a wonderful time. We even had our pre-show prayer time with some of us hanging out the door into the graveyard, but it felt like that passage, Hebrews 12, verse 1, which says, 'As for us, we have a great crowd of witnesses around us. So then, let us rid ourselves of everything that gets in the way, and of the sin which holds on to us so tightly, and let us run with determination the race that lies before us.' Can you hear those that have gone before urging you on?

Riverdance

A preacher was completing a temperance sermon: with great expression he said, 'If I had all the beer in the world, I'd take it and throw it into the river.' With even greater emphasis he said, 'And if I had all the wine in the world, I'd take it and throw it into the river.'

And then finally he said, 'And if I had all the whiskey in the world, I'd take it and throw it into the river.'

He sat down. The song leader then stood very cautiously and announced with a smile, 'For our closing song, let us sing Hymn 365: "Shall We Gather at the River".'

Knock Three Times

A drunk wanders into a Catholic Church and sits down in the confessional box. He says nothing and a few minutes go by. The bewildered priest next door coughs to attract the man's attention, but the drunk still says nothing. The priest then knocks on the wall, once, twice and then a third time, in an attempt to get the man to speak. After a long while the drunk pipes up with the words: 'It's no use knockin' mate, there's no paper in this one either!'

Priorities

 When I first asked God to help me through life, I wanted him to sort everything out in one go, perhaps making me like some sort of spiritual superman. I was living with my partner at the time, and suddenly panicked when I wondered if I should move out immediately. I prayed about it and God said very clearly to me that he had other priorities in my life at that time. It wasn't long before I got married and enjoyed a whole new family, but I will always remember that our priorities aren't always God's.

Reaching the Parts

 They say that beauty is skin deep, but it isn't, because it reaches right down to the very bone. This is what a forensic scientist recently said in a television documentary explaining that she could take a human skull, map out the geology of the bone and then re-create a face around it so that we would know what someone from hundreds of years ago actually looks like. There is a Bible verse, Hebrews 4, verse 12, that says that '. . . the word of God is quick, and powerful, and sharper than any two edged sword, piercing even to the dividing asunder of soul and spirit, and of the joints and marrow

. . .' In other words, God reaches the parts that nothing else can reach.

Food of the Gods

 Apparently the Aztecs called their cacao tree the 'food of the gods'. This is because their tree was the source of chocolate! The Aztecs considered cacao to be man's inheritance from Quetzalcoatl, the god of the air. I agree that it is certainly a wonderful gift of food to be grateful for. I understand that the pioneer John Cadbury was a Christian man and he has been synonymous with chocolate since 1824, when he opened his first shop, establishing a flourishing dynasty that today provides the world with many of its favourite brands of chocolate. I wonder if that's why chocolate and Easter often go together. Next Easter, when I get frustrated at seeing all the chocolate eggs in the shop, I'll remember that. Thank you, Lord!

A Special Thank You

 A Christian was thrown into the ring with a lion. Terrified, he fell on his knees and started praying. At the same time the lion dropped down on its knees and started praying too. The Christian, overjoyed, exclaimed, 'Thank God! Another Christian!' To which the lion replied, 'I don't know about you, but I'm saying Grace.'

I think there is one spiritual tradition that has been used less and less over the years and that is saying Grace. It's a great opportunity for us to remember to say thank you for all that we have been given, and somehow brings a family together around a table. It's interesting to see that in some societies they say Grace after meals too. A double thank you for the gift of food that sustains our lives. What would we do without it?

Hypochondriac's Grace

Fred Moor gave permission to use his wonderful prayer created when he was going back to a family reunion; a very religious group they were. As the 'black sheep of the family' he knew he would be asked to say Grace, so wrote this beforehand. With great sombreness he began reading this poem and saw a few closed eyes pop open, then a chuckle or two, then some outright laughing. I hope it makes you laugh too.

Dear Lord, we ask you if you will,
put your blessing on this meal.
We ask you, Father, if it pleases,
protect us from these new diseases.

Please bless the spinach, and the romaine.
And cleanse it of some lurking ptomaine.
God, bless our ice cream and our cola.
Pray it's not teaming with ebola.

And pray the deli didn't sell us
coleslaw ripe with salmonellus.
We also ask a special blessing;
no botulism in the dressing.

While we regard your higher power,
make sure the devilled eggs aren't sour.
And please, Lord, bless our sirloin tip,
and purge it of *E. Coli*'s grip.

A special blessing on the sherry,
oh Lord, we need no dysentery,
so it not poisons, nor impacts,
or liquefies our lower tracts.

And Lord, make sure no one is able
to get sick and die upon this table.
So bless, Lord, all this food we share.
Insure no deadly virus there.

And once we're full and satiated,
we pray we aren't all contaminated,
and wind up just another toll,
for the Center for Disease Control.

One last thing, Lord, if it's OK,
please hold this blessing that we pray.
For all this fear, and all this fright,
has made us lose our appetite.

Long Life

I think the more you complain, the longer God makes you live. Perhaps that's why the grumbling religious leaders were called Sadducees. Because they were Sad-U-Cee! Sorry!

A Place for Me

If there is one major battle that so many people endure, its self-image. For some reason we don't believe that we are unique or special to anyone, least of all to God. Here's a poem that helps put us back on track:

There is a special place in life,
that needs my humble skill,
A certain job I'm meant to do,
which no one else can fulfil.

The time will be demanding,
and the pay is not too good
And yet I wouldn't change it
for a moment – even if I could.

There is a special place in life,
a goal I must attain,
A dream that I must follow,
because I won't be back again.

There is a mark that I must leave,
however small it seems to be,
A legacy of love for those
who follow after me.

There is a special place in life,
that only I may share,
A little path that bears my name,
awaiting me somewhere.

There is a hand that I must hold,
a word that I must say,
A smile that I must give
for there are tears to blow away.

There is a special place in life
that I was meant to fill
A sunny spot where flowers grow,
upon a windy hill.

There's always a tomorrow and
The best is yet to be,
And somewhere in this world,
I know there is a place for me.

Sex and the City

There seems to be an increasing amount of references to sex these days. I don't think there's anything wrong with sex in itself – after all, it was given to us by God for pro-creation and enjoyment. The problem with it, like with many other things, is when it is abused. We can abuse our bodies, minds and spirits in many different ways, perhaps by over-eating, smoking or even when we don't get enough sleep. The guidelines for life that God has given us are more for our own safety and to avoid hurting others, than because it upsets God. It's not always easy, though, and God really understands when we get it wrong. We are surrounded and pressured by a huge amount of temptation and desire in our world, something that was not there in Jesus' time. If you are in a position of having an affair or in a relationship you know isn't right, whatever you do, don't shut God out. Let him in, ask him to help you, and he will gently carry you back to a place where he can bring you healing and help. Remember Psalm 42: 'He pulled me out of a dangerous pit, out of the deadly quicksand. He set me safely on a rock and made me secure.'

Desire

I like the way that Dr Purnell puts it when he says:

Each of us has five significant parts in our lives. We have the physical, the emotional, the mental, the social, and the spiritual. All five of these parts are designed to work together in harmony. In our search for intimacy we want the solution today, or yesterday. One of our problems is that we want 'instant' gratification. When the need for intimacy in a relationship is not met, we look for an 'instant' solution. Where do we look? Physical, mental, social, emotional or spiritual? It's the physical. It is easier to be physically intimate with someone than to be intimate in any of the other four areas. You can become physically intimate with a person of the opposite sex in an hour, or half-hour – it just depends upon the urge! But you soon discover that sex may only be a temporary relief for a superficial desire. There is a much deeper need that is still unmet.

It's easy to mistake what we want as sex when really it's intimacy. This is why I believe sex works best and is the most satisfying in the context of marriage. It's not that God is a spoilsport, he just knows and desires what is best for us.

Three Little Pigs

 Jokes often have a serious hidden meaning and sometimes it's great fun seeing if you can find it. This lovely little story always makes me laugh and reminds me that if you are feeling like the odd one out, you are still greatly loved.

Three Little Pigs went out to dinner one night. The waiter came and took their drink order.

'I would like a Sprite,' said the first little piggy.

'I would like a Coke,' said the second little piggy.

'I want beer, lots and lots of beer,' said the third little piggy.

The drinks were brought out and the waiter took their orders for dinner.

'I want a nice big steak,' said the first piggy.

'I would like the salad plate,' said the second piggy.

'I want beer, lots and lots of beer,' said the third little piggy.

The meals were brought out and a while later the waiter approached the table and asked if the piggies would like any dessert.

'I want a banana split,' said the first piggy.

'I want a cheesecake,' said the second piggy.

'I want beer, lots and lots of beer,' exclaimed the third little piggy.

'Pardon me for asking,' said the waiter to the third little piggy,'

But why have you only ordered beer all evening?'

The third piggy says, 'Well, somebody has to go "Wee, wee, wee, all the way home!"'

The Right Finale

Don't wait for six strong men to take you to church.

Love Is All Around

This is a beautiful love poem from God, but we will only hear him read it to us if we can listen:

Love, the greatest gift anyone can have,
Love descends upon us from the heavens,
God is speaking, are you listening?

Be silent, my child, and hear the voice within,
Like a flowing river, falling rain, a thunderous roar,
Hear me now for I am God.

I dwell within you and am here to stay,
Listen to my music or let it play.
I will always wait for you, here within,
My love is free I will never take it away.

Never look outside, for I dwell within,
Never fear again, I'll always be here.
Just listen to my voice, in the start like the rain
And then like an orchestra.

Hear me now.

Come on, Guys!

I'm told that women laugh on average 18 times a day, so maybe that's why they live longer? Guys don't laugh half that much, and so we've obviously got some catching up to do!

Ten Commandments

Ten things about us that prove God has a wonderful sense of humour:

1 It's impossible to sneeze with your eyes open.
2 The average person falls asleep in seven minutes.
3 It is physically impossible to lick your elbow.
4 Our eyes are always the same size from birth, but our ears and noses don't stop growing.

5 People say 'Bless you' when you sneeze, but did you know that when you do, your heart stops for a millisecond?

6 In the course of an average lifetime you will, while sleeping, eat 70 assorted insects and 10 spiders.

7 Like fingerprints, everyone's tongue print is different.

8 Every human spent about half an hour as a single cell.

9 On average, half of all false teeth have some form of radioactivity.

10 Over 75 per cent of people who read this will try to lick their elbow!

A Tenner's Worth

 Ten facts about God's Creation that remind me to enjoy life even more:

1 The oldest known goldfish lived to 41 years of age. Its name was Fred.

2 If an orang-utan belches at you, watch out. He's warning you to stay out of his territory.

3 A shark is the only fish that can blink with both eyes.

4 There are more chickens than people in the world.

5 A dragonfly has a life span of 24 hours.

6 A goldfish has a memory span of three seconds, and a pregnant goldfish is called a twit.

7 Elephants are the only animals that can't jump.

8 It is possible to lead a cow upstairs, but not downstairs.

9 A snail can sleep for three years.

10 An ostrich's eye is bigger than its brain.

Upside-down God

You can't impress God, and believe me I've tried! He's got the T-shirt, you see, and knows all of our foibles and imperfections, but still accepts us just as we are.

That's why he's an inside-out, upside-down God, because he looks at things in a completely different way to us. If someone ever asks me a question I can't answer, I simply say that I don't know. I'm not embarrassed, as if I should know everything, because if I did know I would be God. Isaiah 55, verse 8, says, 'My thoughts,' says the Lord, 'are not like yours, and my ways are different from yours.' That's quite a relief to me because it means I can leave all the answers to him.

Free Valuation

It's important to remind ourselves that self-esteem is different from pride and that our sense of being a good person of worth should not depend on what we do, even if we are working for God. We get self-worth and esteem by having a relationship with God, and asking him to put right any bad examples we had from our earthly parents. We can know we are valuable because of the high price God paid for us with the death of his Son, Jesus Christ. It's not wrong to feel good about ourselves. When we experience earthly things, endorphins – the so-called 'feel-good' chemicals – are released in our brains and we feel a brief surge of energy and pleasure. When you feel a sense of well-being it is because of the way that God designed you. Thank him for that.

Older but Wiser

Funny things happen to you when you get older, as I've recently been discovering. Fortunately, I know that I'm well on the train to heaven so it's something I try to laugh about as much as possible, as I do when I read this poem:

How do I know my youth has been spent:
Because my get-up-and-go, got up and went
But in spite of all that, I'm able to grin
When I think where my get-up-and-go has been

Old age is golden, I've heard it said,
But sometimes I wonder as I go to bed
My ears are in a drawer, my teeth in a cup,
My eyes on a table until I wake up

When I was young my slippers were red
I could kick my heels right over my head
When I grew older my slippers were blue
But I could still dance the whole night thru

Now that I am old my slippers are black
I walk to the corner and puff my way back
The reason I know my youth is spent
My get-up-and-go got up and went

I get up each morning dust off my wits
Pick up the paper and read the 'obits'
If my name is missing, I know I'm not dead
So I eat a good breakfast and go back to bed.

Granny Says

We used to laugh at Gran and the things she would say about her husband getting old, such as 'You're not going bald, your hair is just relocating!' Or, 'You're not going bald, your head is just getting bigger!' I do wish we showed more respect in this country to the older generation for they are the ones with years of experience behind them, and I think we have so much to learn if we take the time to listen.

Fairer Sex

Women make up 70 per cent of the world, which is fine by me, and here's a prayer especially for them:

Now I lay me
Down to sleep
I pray the Lord
My shape to keep
Please no wrinkles
Please no bags
And please lift my bum
Before it sags
Please no age spots
Please no grey
And as for my belly,
Please take it away
Please keep me healthy
Please keep me young
And thank you, dear Lord
For all that you've done
Amen.

Spread a Smile

 Eva Fraser from The Facial Workout Studio says, 'People who regularly exercise their face muscles can expect to delay middle aged sagging for at least ten years.' I realized that was cheaper than botox, so I went on a mission the other day and, as I walked up the street, I made sure I smiled at everyone who passed me. The different responses were amazing. Sometimes people scowled at me, sometimes they ignored me, but sometimes they smiled back. Christians have a lot to smile about, and yet we have the reputation for doing completely the opposite. Go on, exercise those muscles today, help to get the world smiling, and look ten years younger in the process!

Encouragement

 Showbiz has always looked far more glamorous on the outside than it really is. It's often a cruel and lonely world in which it is difficult to make a success of yourself. If you are alone, it is sometimes hard to survive in such a world. Tommy and I have been very fortunate that our comic partnership was recognized early on and that we are still going strong more than 40 years later. We are both grateful for the support that the charity Christians In Entertainment has given us over the years, and everything it continues to do today. It bases its backstage work on Hebrews 10, verse 25, which I think has deep implications for all of us: 'Let us not give up the habit of meeting together, as some are doing. Instead, let us encourage one another all the more, since you see that the Day of the Lord is coming nearer.' Meeting together and encouragement. Sounds like it could be a little taste of heaven.

Nicodemus Work

 From a weekly group on *Phantom of the Opera* in London's West End, to the hundreds of backstage visits it makes all over the country, the Bibles placed in the dressing rooms, and the prayer-line that is there to help to support those working away from family, friends and church, the charity Christians In Entertainment has a vital mission in helping to keep the spiritual side of showbiz alive. It's a bit like a spiritual 'meals-on-wheels' service, but I call it a 'Secret-Service work' because there is another side to Christians In Entertainment that few are privy to. Like Nicodemus who popped in secretly to see Jesus in the middle of the night for fear of being recognized, part of Christians In Entertainment's work is meeting up with many well-known names in the entertainment business who want to ask questions about God and faith, but they need to do it quietly and in strict confidence without the intrusion of the press. Christians In Entertainment celebrates 25 years of this secret-service backstage support in 2007, and I know that many churches will be praying that this spiritual work will reach deeper and wider with the love of God. So, when you next watch your television, listen to a CD or see a live show, don't forget to send a prayer up for all those working in the world of entertainment.

Bible Hit Parade

If some of the characters from the Bible had to audition for the *X-Factor*, I think they would sing:

Noah: 'Raindrops Keep Falling on My Head'
Adam and Eve: 'Strangers in Paradise'
Esther: 'I Feel Pretty'
Job: 'Birth of the Blues'
Moses: 'The Wanderer'
Jezebel: 'The Lady is a Tramp'
Samson: 'Hair'
Salome: 'I Could Have Danced All Night'
Daniel: 'The Lion King'
Joshua: 'Good Vibrations'
Esau: 'Born To Be Wild'
Shadrach, Meshach and Abednego: 'Stayin' Alive'
The Three Kings: 'When You Wish Upon a Star'
Elijah: 'Up, Up, and Away'
Nebuchadnezzar: 'Crazy'

New Charges

A television evangelist in the USA recently made a joke announcement that: '. . . God's Direct Hotline is being closed down permanently. No longer will God hear or allow prayers direct from consumers. Henceforth all requests and entreaties of God must be passed through one of God's licensed and appointed earthly emissaries.' Apparently Falwell himself was to be in overall charge of the new program.

'There will be of course a small fee involved for each contact,' said Falwell. 'A petitioner who does not have the money must try to raise it from family or friends, or, if credit worthy, may be allowed to borrow the amount from one of our approved lenders at nominal interest rates. Should a petitioner be in default more than two prayers' worth, he or she shall be excommunicated until the financial default is cured. Severe defaults shall result in public stonings or floggings, so all are hereby warned to keep their accounts fully paid up. That's the only way we will be able to operate this new program successfully, and in accordance with God's will.'

Phew, what a good thing he was only joking! It makes me grateful to remember just how easy it is to pray.

The New 23rd Psalm

 In such a fast changing world of increasing sophistication and jargon, I'm sure that in a few years a new version of the Bible will have been produced that incorporates much of this modernistic language. The 23rd Psalm could never be the same again. It may sound something like this:

The Lord and I are in a shepherd–sheep situation, and I am in a position of negative need.

He prostrates me in a greenbelt grazing area, and conducts me directionally parallel to a non-torrential aqueous liquid.

He restores to original satisfaction levels my psychological make-up.

Notwithstanding the fact that I make ambulatory progress through the non-illuminated inter-hill mortality slot, terror sensations shall not be observed within me due to the proximity of the omnipotence.

Your pastoral walking aid and quadruped pick-up unit introduce me to a pleasurific mood state.

You design and produce a nutrient-bearing furniture-type structure in the context of non-cooperative elements, and my beverage utensil experiences a volume crisis.

You enact ahead related folk ritual utilizing vegetable extracts.

Surely it must be an ongoing non-deductible fact that your inter-relational, emphatical and non-vengeful capacities will pursue me as their target focus for the duration of this non-death period.

And I will possess tenant rights in the housing unit of the Lord on a permanently open-ended time-basis.

Thank goodness that God is the same, yesterday, today and for ever!

I've Started So I'll Finish

 I don't feel I'm getting older on the inside, but I have to admit to a few joints being a bit creakier these days. This is a letter I might find myself writing to my children in the years to come:

Just a line to say I'm living
that I'm not among the dead,
Though I'm getting more forgetful
and mixed up in my head.

I got used to my arthritis
to my dentures I'm resigned,
I can manage my bifocals
but God, I miss my mind,

For sometimes I can't remember
when I stand at the foot of the stairs,
if I must go up for something
or have I just come down from there?

And before the fridge so often
my poor mind is filled with doubt,
Have I just put food away, or
have I come to take some out?

And there's a time when it is dark
with my nightcap on my head,
I don't know if I'm retiring, or
just getting out of bed

So, if it's my turn to write you
there's no need for getting sore,
I may think I have written
and don't want to be a bore.

So, remember that I love you
and wish that you were near,
But now it's nearly mail time
So I must say goodbye, dear,

There I stand beside the mail box
with a face so very red,
instead of mailing you my letter
I opened it instead!

Alpha and Omega

Alpha and Omega are the first and last letters of the Greek Alphabet, similar to referring to someone in English as 'the A to Z'. God is called this in the Bible because he is there when I wake up and he's there when I go to sleep. It reminds me of this wonderful old hymn:

Great is Thy faithfulness, O God my Father;
There is no shadow of turning with Thee;
Thou changest not, Thy compassions, they fail not;
As Thou hast been, Thou forever will be.

Great is Thy faithfulness!
Great is Thy faithfulness!
Morning by morning new mercies I see.
All I have needed Thy hand hath provided;
Great is Thy faithfulness, Lord, unto me!

Summer and winter and springtime and harvest,
Sun, moon and stars in their courses above
Join with all nature in manifold witness
To Thy great faithfulness, mercy and love.

Pardon for sin and a peace that endureth
Thine own dear presence to cheer and to guide;
Strength for today and bright hope for tomorrow,
Blessings all mine, with ten thousand beside!

Goodnight Prayer

May God support us all the day long
till the shadows lengthen
and the evening comes
and the busy world is hushed
and the fever of life is over
and our work is done –
then in mercy –
may God give us a safe lodging
and a holy rest
and peace at the last.
Amen.

The Future Is Bright

Tommy started, so I'll finish. I think it's always good to end with a prayer and a laugh while placing our futures in God's hands, so here is my prayer for you:

May you get a clean bill of health from your dentist, your cardiologist, your gastro-endocrinologist, your urologist, your proctologist, your podiatrist, your psychiatrist, your gynaecologist, your plumber, and the Inland Revenue.

May your hair, your teeth, your face-lift, your abs, and your stocks not fall; and may your blood pressure, your triglycerides, your cholesterol, your white blood count, and your mortgage interest not rise.

May you find a way to travel from anywhere to anywhere in the rush hour in less than an hour, and when you get there may you find a parking space.

May December 31st find you seated around the dinner table, together with your beloved family and cherished friends, ushering in the New Year ahead. You will find the food better, the environment quieter, the cost much cheaper, and the pleasure much more fulfilling than anything else you might ordinarily do that night.

May you wake up on January 1st, finding that the world has not come to an end, the lights work, the water taps flow, and the sky has not fallen in.

May you go to the bank on the morning of January 3rd and find your account is in order, your money is still there and any mistakes are in your favour.

May you ponder on January 4th, 'How did this ultra modern civilization of ours manage to get itself traumatized by a possible slip of a blip on a chip made out of sand?'

May you relax about the future and realize that you still have a long long time until you pass, by which time the computer is long since obsolete and so are you.

May God give you the strength to go through a year of political campaigning and may some of the promises made be kept.

May you be awe-struck by God's sense of humour as you look in the mirror each morning. May what you see in the mirror delight you, and what others see in you delight them.

May someone love you enough to forgive your faults, be blind to your blemishes, and tell the world about your virtues.

May the telesales people wait to make their calls until you finish dinner, and may your cheque book and your budget balance, and may they include generous amounts for charity.

May you remember to say 'I love you' at least once a day to your spouse, your child, your parents, your friends; but not to your secretary, your nurse, your personal trainer, your hairdresser, or your tennis coach.

May we live as God intended, in a world at peace and the awareness of His love in every sunset, every flower's unfolding petals, every baby's smile, every lover's kiss, and every wonderful, astonishing, miraculous beat of our heart.
Amen.

Acknowledgements

The brilliantly funny original cartoons in this volume are by John Byrne, best known for his work with *Private Eye* and his '*Dear John . . .*' column in *The Stage* newspaper, as well as live appearances on *Nickelodeon* and *CBeebies* television, and as BBC London's Late Night Agony Uncle. Thanks, John!

Bobby and Tommy are grateful for all the stories sent to them to be included in this book. While every effort has been made to contact the copyright holders of material used, this has not always been successful. Full acknowledgement will gladly be made in future editions. With particular thanks to Endtime Poetry (www.loriswebs.com/endtimepoetry) and Timothy Jon Barrett for 'Spiritual Amnesia'.

Tommy would like to thank his wife Hazel, and Bobby his wife Yvonne, for being such a support to them both throughout the ups and downs of a showbiz life.

Chris would like to thank Maggie and Tony for the seafront hospitality which offered much tranquillity during the personal bumpy months of writing this book. Also to Kath and Andy, Charlie and Sue, Michael and Carole, Keith and Christine for their special friendship and support, recently discovering how valuable true friendship is. Also for the extra prayer support of Sally Goring, Mike Doyle, Dave and Karen Berry, Lin and Jan Bennett, Diane Regan,

Margaret Spencer, Ruth and Ivan, and the trustees Nick, Mike, Glyn and Bill for keeping him going. Chris would also like to say that he is grateful to his children Luke, Anna and Ben for making him so proud of them all.

Chris Gidney

Chris comes from a showbusiness family, and at the age of nine formed a comedy magic double-act with his father. Since then he has spent a lifetime in the profession as entertainer, producer and author, working with numerous artistes from the legendary Frank Sinatra to Sir Cliff Richard. Joining London's West End in 1980, he enjoyed 12 consecutive productions before moving to BBC Television, working on such classic programmes as *Blue Peter* and *That's Life* with Esther Rantzen.

Based on his extensive friendships within the profession, his first book, *In the Limelight*, was published in 1993 by HarperCollins, and since then he has written 27 books covering various aspects of life in showbusiness. Chris's hardbacks include the best-selling *Celebrating Secombe* for Sir Harry Secombe; *Rock on Tommy* for Cannon & Ball; *Under No Illusion* for Paul Daniels; *Vicar to Dad's Army* with Frank Williams; *Flying High* and *Closer to Heaven* for BBC Radio 2's Don Maclean; *Little by Little* with Syd Little; *Tapestry Tales* with Dora Bryan; and *Show Me the Way* with Wendy Craig. Chris's *Long Hot Soak* series was sold out before it even arrived in the shops, and he has also written for BBC radio and a number of newspapers and periodicals.

As a freelance director and producer he is responsible for a number of unique stage, television and radio productions, while his recording company, *Fusion*, has produced several music, audio and video releases. In 2004 he co-founded That's Entertainment Productions, which specializes in bringing high-quality family entertainment to the commercial theatre. That's Entertainment Productions has several productions on the road at any one time.

Chris formed the showbusiness charity Christians In Entertainment in 1982. This continues to provide backstage spiritual support for professionals in the entertainment industry, and he remains the director of this organization. Chris has a grown-up family and enjoys living in the South-East.

For information on the charity Christians in Entertainment, please visit our website at: www.cieweb.org.uk.

For details on how to book Bobby and Tommy's Gospel Show and other Christian entertainers with a faith to share, please visit the website: www.shorehillarts. co.uk.

For details of John Byrne's column, e-mail him at: Dearjohn@thestage.co.uk.